THE DOGS

Laura Thompson was born in Bedfordshire in 1964. On leaving Oxford University she worked as an actress and a director, including the staging of a one-woman show about the life of Jean Rhys, played by herself. She has written a regular sports column for *The Times*, and is now a contributing editor of *Esquire* magazine.

CW00952393

Laura Thompson

THE DOGS

A Personal History
of Greyhound Racing

Published by Vintage 1995

2 4 6 8 10 9 7 5 3 1

Copyright © Laura Thompson 1994

The right of Laura Thompson to be identified as the
author of this work has been asserted by her in accor-
dance with the Copyright, Designs and Patents Act, 1988

First published in Great Britain by
Chatto & Windus Ltd, 1994

Vintage
Random House, 20 Vauxhall Bridge Road, London SW1V 2SA

Random House Australia (Pty) Limited
20 Alfred Street, Milsons Point, Sydney
New South Wales 2061, Australia

Random House New Zealand Limited
18 Poland Road, Glenfield,
Auckland 10, New Zealand

Random House South Africa (Pty) Limited
PO Box 337, Bergvlei, South Africa

Random House UK Limited Reg. No. 954009

A CIP catalogue record for this book
is available from the British Library

ISBN 0 09 944871 8

Printed and bound in Great Britain by
The Guernsey Press Co. Ltd., Guernsey, Channel Islands

TO MY FATHER; AND TO ALL THE DOGS

Acknowledgements

Without my father, this book would not have been written. For their kindness and help I should like to thank Geoffrey Thomas and Frank Melville at the NGRC; Ann Aslett and all the Chandler family at Walthamstow stadium; Roy James; Johanna Beumer; Jonathan Burnham; Mark Bell; and my mother. I am also very grateful to Paul Duffett and to Bob Betts, editor of *The Greyhound Life*, for lending me several of the photographs that are reproduced here.

Picture Credits

Page 1, top *The Greyhound Life*; bottom Walthamstow Stadium.

Page 2, top *The Greyhound Life*, photo by Paul Duffett; bottom *The Greyhound Life*.

Page 3, top *The Greyhound Life*, photo by Gale; bottom *The Greyhound Life*.

Page 4, top *The Greyhound Life*; middle Belle Vue Stadium; bottom *The Greyhound Life*.

Contents

Note: Asterisks refer to the Notes
at the back of the book.

I

Facts

The simple facts are these. Six greyhounds run around
an ovoid track in pursuit of a mechanical hare. The
hare always wins. It is the mystery of what will come
second that fascinates those who go to the dogs.

The greyhounds wear jackets whose colours, like
jockeys' silks, help one to separate a dog from the
tangled knot, the brief blur of bodies: trap one – red;
trap two – blue; trap three – white; trap four – black;
trap five – orange; trap six – black-white stripes. But
only in gambling extremis is a greyhound just a number.
They have names, they have identities, they have
characters, and they have histories: these, too, help to
separate them from the tangled knot.

Six nights a week and six afternoons a week, every
week of the year, people are going to the dogs and betting on the dogs. About £400 million a year is gambled
on the dogs on-course, at the tracks, and about £1,600
million a year is gambled off-course, in the betting
shops. Every day, twelve or more greyhound tracks
stage meetings that comprise ten or twelve races. This
means that on, let us say, 312 days a year, on *every one* of
those days, up to 1,000 greyhounds will be put into tiny

traps to wait, scrabbling and howling, for the hare to make its circuit, for the moment when it will pass the traps, when the doors will be snapped open and they can spring out after it. Every year in Britain alone, never mind Ireland, America, Mexico, Australia and Spain, around 50,000 greyhound races are run; every year, dogs are put into those traps over a quarter of a million times. What other sport gives itself to its public in such continuous abundance? There are no seasons in greyhound racing, no rests from the world. The dogs never closes.

Most of the 50,000 or so annual races in Britain are what one might call the roughage of the sport, run for a winner's prize of less than £100 by dogs of ordinary ability over one circuit of the track. These are known as graded races. The vast majority of greyhounds are graders. Until the late 1970s, the calibre of a graded race was gauged by the amount of prize money that it offered; now, however, races are graded by number, usually from one to nine, with nine being for pups and scrubbers, one for fliers. It is the track's racing manager who decides what grade of race a dog should run in. He also has to assign, as well as is possible, the right dog to the right trap. Some greyhounds, no one really knows why, like to run on the inside, close to the rails, while others – known as wide runners – like to be on the outside, clear of the other dogs. The racing manager will draw a railer in trap one or two and a wide runner in trap five or six, but the problems come with traps three and four, the 'death' traps, in which, unless a dog is rather lucky or rather superior, it may find itself impossibly sandwiched between two thick chunks of greyhound. A racing manager who draws a dog continually in either of these traps will be accused by its owner of pursuing a vendetta, whilst he who draws a dog too often in trap one or six will be accused by the other five owners of favouritism. His is a complicated and thankless task. It cannot be otherwise; for it is of the essence of greyhound racing that too many dogs should be attempting to negotiate a too sharply shaped track. Otherwise the fastest dog would win every time; and where would that leave everyone?

Some tracks practise handicap racing, often with eight dogs. The traps are staggered as in an athletics event, which means that, in theory, each greyhound gets a clear run. Handicapping is still relatively rare in Britain. It is far more common in Australia, where at least eight, and sometimes as many as ten, dogs compete in each race – the best racing manager in the world could not get that many dogs running smoothly from level traps. In truth, handicapping is a fairer system than the bumping, scuffling, shut-your-eyes-and-pray-your-dog-made-it-round-the-bend one that operates at the majority of British tracks. But greyhound racing is a traditionalist sport, and it remains loyal to the imperfect but trusted method of racing that it has always known.

A few tracks are, nonetheless, so tight and sharply bended that decent racing is almost impossible. They vary considerably in shape and size, but an average race, of a little over one circuit, is about 470 metres. This takes something less than thirty seconds to cover and is the distance that most greyhounds have been bred to run; known as four-bend races, these are denoted by an 'A' in a race programme (for example, A1, A9). Rarer than these are the 'S' races, the six benders, run over 1¾ circuits of the track, races of about 650 metres and forty seconds. Six-bend dogs are preferred by wiser owners, because they give you more of a run for your money. They can be drawn in trap three, miss their break from the traps, fill a greyhound sandwich for half a minute and still win a race; whereas if a four-bend dog doesn't get out and away pretty smartly, then as often as not it might as well, as my father puts it, 'be running against spaniels'.

Rarer yet than the six-bend races are sprints, races of about 250 metres and fifteen seconds, for dogs which spurt and fizzle like fireworks; middle distance races of about 550 metres and thirty-five seconds; marathons of about 800 metres and fifty-three seconds; and hurdle races. These times are extremely rough estimates – the difference between a scrubby and a classy dog can be two seconds or more. But however slow a greyhound might be, it is still effortlessly fast compared with a human athlete. Even an A9 dog will run at something approaching forty miles an hour.

Around ninety per cent of greyhounds are graders, running out their two or three years of working life in races that will be almost immediately forgotten. But then there are those dogs – oh so rare, oh so precious – that, on a glorious day in their lives, will suddenly reveal themselves too good for A1 and S1 races, will streak laughingly away from their graded opposition, and will be unable to be placed by a racing manager because they will win every time they run at even money*. What do you do with them? You take them open racing. If graded races are the roughage of the sport, then opens are the glucose. They can be anything from a local-bookmaker-sponsored romp round Milton Keynes track for £100 and a silver-plated, six-inch greyhound, to the *Daily Mirror*-sponsored Derby at Wimbledon stadium for £40,000 and a huge, elegant trophy – although the Derby is not merely an open race, it is a Classic, one of the ten British races* which form the peaks of the sport. Below these heights, open races are frequent – hardly a night goes by without at least one open – but tracks, trainers and punters always want more of them, because they put glamour and fun into that stalwart daily show. And owners, of course, always yearn for open race dogs. But they are hard to find, or at least hard to buy, unless one is lucky enough to get an untried pup that then makes a magical metamorphosis. To buy a decent greyhound over the age of eighteen months, whose puppy form implies that it might turn into even a minor open racer, will cost perhaps £8,000. A dog that might make a major open racer will almost always cost five figures.

There are several ways of buying a greyhound. One might get it from a breeder – usually in Ireland – or from an agent, a trainer, an auction or the back pages of *The Greyhound Life**; one might get it as a baby or as a fully known quantity. Nothing ensures success, although knowing a good breeder is probably the safest method. However, these people are not so easy to get in with. One cannot just cruise into their kennels, waving a blank cheque, and cruise out again with an impeccably bred, blunt-footed little creature that in a year's time will be dancing its way through the Derby trials. With breeders, as with everything in greyhound racing, one has to be *in the know*. It is only those that are in the know that have any real chance of consistent success; in the know is the elusive, slippery place where every dog man strives to be. Being in the know is, to dog racing, like wearing an MCC tie to a cricket lover, or meeting a Wimbledon debenture holder to a tennis lover, or joining the Bullingdon to an Oxford undergraduate, or getting backstage with the Rolling Stones to a groupie. Its desirability is absolute, sensual, indestructible, ineffable.

But say you have your greyhound – A9er, open racer, 500 quid's worth, sold your car to buy it, whatever. Then you place it with a trainer. There are people who train their own dogs, and there are private trainers who handle only open racers, but the majority of trainers are attached to a track, with charge of some of the graders that run at that track and, possibly, of some open race dogs as well. Each track has between seven and twelve trainers contracted to it.

Before a greyhound can race at a track, it will have a minimum of three trials, in which it will race with up to three other dogs until it is fast enough to be accepted on to the racecard. Usually, the more upmarket the stadium, the faster the grading time, the better the racing and the higher the prize money. At a top London track like Walthamstow, low grade dogs win about £50 per race, top grade up to about £100; at a middle grade, provincial track like Oxford, the corresponding figures would be about £35 and £70. Even the last dog in a race will get between about £10 and £20.

Compared with other countries, this prize money is extraordinarily low. In America and Australia it is perhaps three or four times as high, although they do have far fewer meetings, often only one a week per track. But however many meetings a track has, a dog would never run more than once a week, so British owners cannot make up the deficit. Here, unless a race is sponsored, the prize money will be minimal. At £25 or £35 a week, however, a dog is very cheap to keep, so if it wins occasionally and stays fit, it can quite easily pay for itself. But it is impossible to *make* much money out of a graded greyhound unless your prize money is supplemented by astute gambling. A good open racer, however, will earn wads of prize money, shelf-fuls of silverware, delicious hoards of gambling returns and perhaps, if male, thousands of pounds' worth of stud fees. It will cost about £100 to buy the services of an unproven stud dog. One that has already thrown good pups will cost £400 or more, and will be fighting off all the females that eager breeders throw at him. But no less precious than such a virile creature is the brood bitch that produces his litter; the breeder with the bitch that consistently throws fine pups has a woman whose price is above rubies.

There are currently thirty-seven licensed tracks in Britain* (twenty-one in Ireland; forty-seven in America, of which eighteen are in Florida; and ninety in Australia, of which forty-six are in New South Wales). There are also, in Britain, about fifty 'flapping' or unlicensed tracks. For a track to be licensed it must operate under the jurisdiction of the National Greyhound Racing Club (NGRC), which has regulated the dogs since 1928. In Eire the regulatory body is the Bord na gCon; in Ulster it is the Irish Coursing Club, which also registers every greyhound bred in Ireland. All licensed British tracks are subject to stringent NGRC controls, the purpose of which is to limit corruption in dog racing. For example, to ensure no rogue gambler can spike it with an untoward snack or aperitif, before racing every dog will be weighed, dope tested and kennelled under supervision. If for some mysterious reason – of which more later – it still runs at wild variance from its previous form, finding or losing chunks of seconds, then the NGRC 'flying squad' may swoop in and have it dope tested *after* the race as well. The NGRC can also order the trainer to appear before its stewards and talk himself out of trouble.

The dope testing, which is very similar to that of athletes and is done on a urine sample, is the most visible of the NGRC's activities. Of course the body does other things as well. It registers every greyhound that races in Britain (and helps fund itself by charging their owners*); it has the power to give and retract trainers' licences; it can ban any unfit owner or miscreant track official; and it tries to enforce the rule that forbids track officials and trainers from gambling. In this last it fails almost completely. More precisely, it succeeds in enforcing the letter of the law; but even if one may not gamble in person, one may still find some kind man willing to do so for one. Nevertheless, the NGRC must be seen to be trying to regulate even the ungovernable areas of its sport. It is a necessary and respectable body, fighting a Sisyphian battle against the common perception of dog racing as a crooked business. It does its job extremely well, although insiders tend to regard it with the grudging, schoolboyish resentment with which footballers view referees, and outsiders have no idea that anything like it exists.

For outsiders seem to think that all greyhound tracks are like flapping tracks: unlicensed, unrestricted, pullulating with corruption and with men in camel coats pulling fast ones. There *are* tracks like that. There used to be a lot more of them. But there is a real track hierarchy in greyhound racing, and the similarity between a flapping track like Bedwelty and a superior stadium like Walthamstow is as remote as that between an A9 dog and a Derby winner. The strokes that are so easy to pull at the flaps, where dogs are neither weighed nor dope tested nor, sometimes, who their owners say they are, are comparably difficult to pull at a licensed track – though, of course, to some people all rules are there to be broken. Greyhound racing, like any business, harbours corruption. But this element is disproportionately magnified by the public, who seem almost to *want* to see the dogs as being fly as a £4 note.

Between the wild frontier of the flaps and the ordered heartland of the licensees are what are called permit tracks, like Milton Keynes and Canterbury. Trainers with a permit, rather than a full licence, are only allowed to handle greyhounds that they themselves own; there *are* fully licensed trainers attached to permit tracks, but the majority run tiny, personal organisations, such as the one owned by a friend of my father, which had flying ducks on the wall of each kennel. Permit tracks operate under the NGRC, but they are not always as stringently run as this moral guardianship might imply. They are downmarket, intimate little hotbeds of familiarity. The standards they maintain are comfortable, cynically realistic, compared with the stately way in which the top tracks try to conduct themselves. Despite the fact that permit track dogs are dope tested and kennelled under supervision, they often run way off form. Far less frequently, an orchestrated scam will try to engineer the outcome of a race by knocking out more than one of the six greyhounds (then going on to place large sums of money – carefully distributed around several betting shops – on some unlikely 5/1 shot). Strokes as bold as this are common in flapping but are far more difficult to pull at a licensed track. This is why they are, indeed, rare; and why their discovery always causes such a furore in the greyhound press. How many remain undiscovered is, of course, unknown.

The dodgy race is a perpetual hazard for betting shops. Sometimes, if they suspect what is going on, they can, pending an inquiry, refuse to pay out, but sometimes, inevitably, they get caught. This is particularly painful for them if the race in question is run at a BAGS

(Bookmakers' Afternoon Greyhound Services) meeting, as more money is wagered on afternoon than evening dog racing. Several tracks provide both afternoon and evening meetings, and Hackney, for example, is almost exclusively a BAGS track. There has always been afternoon dog racing – during the Second World War that was all there was, and after that a few tracks still only opened during the day – but when betting shops were legalised in 1961, attendances at these meetings naturally fell, and daytime racing ceased to be self-supporting. However the bookmakers needed it to continue for their betting shops, and in 1967 they formed BAGS, whose purpose was to ensure an afternoon racing service by giving a sum of money to the NGRC, which would then be distributed to the relevant tracks. It was, if you like, the way in which the bookmakers recompensed greyhound racing for stealing its customers.

Still at the tracks themselves there are, as there always have been, the on-course bookmakers: Aaron Kelly, Del 'Boy', Peter O'Toole, all the likely lads, standing, as they always have done, in their line of six or seven, by the tracks, on the terraces, streetwise brains clicking like the rosaries of nuns on speed. For their pitch they give the track five times the admission fee for the enclosure in which they stand (so in theory they might only pay a tenner), but they often make additional, beneficent contributions. The richer bookmakers, those who also have betting shops, say, or country mansions in Wanstead, but who never lose the love of standing trackside at night, frequently sponsor races.

For anyone a little fearful of bookmakers – all that shrewd-eyed, give-you-the-hurry-up, terrorising worldliness – and for anyone who prefers to keep their bets beneath the level at which sums of money acquire the names of animals*, prefers, indeed, to place their bets in coins rather than notes, there is, instead, the Tote. It used to be that Tote operators would manually punch your chosen dog's number on to the ticket and would, post-racing, count and check every one of these tickets. Now, of course, the whole thing is computerised and placing a bet doesn't make that lovely satisfying sound which gave such weight to the whole transaction. Every Tote bet goes into a pool from which the stadium takes a certain percentage. In 1934, when the Tote was first legalised at the dogs, this was 6 per cent; in 1970 greyhound racing attendances were falling so badly that it was increased to 12½ per cent; and now a track can take between 20 and 29 per cent, depending on whether the bet is a win, a place* or a forecast*. However, so large a cream-off by the track cannot help but be noticed by the punter and can therefore be self-defeating. The punter may sulk and not bet with the Tote. Most tracks today elect not to take the full percentage to which they are entitled.

In 1948 the Government imposed a 10 per cent tax on Tote betting, on top of the 6 per cent which was already being imposed by the tracks. All that agony, all that studying of the form, and then to win about tuppence! And in 1960, a 5 per cent tax was introduced for on-course bookmaker bets. When betting shops opened the following year, the tax on bets placed with them was

6 per cent; what was an extra 1 per cent compared with all that comfort and convenience? The off-course betting tax did subsequently rise to 10 per cent. But it was not until 1987, when the then Chancellor of the Exchequer Nigel Lawson, in the spirit of largesse with which he was possessed at the time, abolished the tax on both Tote and on-course bets, that the stadia became truly desirable places at which to gamble. From then on, a bet worth having was only worth having at the track. Nip into Walthamstow for an hour and back your good thing there – don't pay 10 per cent on top of your stake into the pocket of William Hill.*

A night greyhound racing need not, of course, be merely Tote or bookmaker. It used to be that the track, the race and the bet were all that was wanted. But after the War, when attendances began a steady and irreversible decline (accelerated, but not wholly caused by, heavy betting taxes), stadia began to realise that they could no longer rely on the fact that crowds of people would always want, simply, to go to the dogs. They began to fashion restaurants, bars, images of other nights out, from the hitherto functional structures that were the stadia. These became, and remain, hierarchical edifices, in which the noblesse sits on high behind tables, behind glass, placing its dainty sums of superfluous change with the Tote or, better still, with the girl who comes to its tables to take its money to the Tote, and stares down at the proletariat as it swarms and seethes around the terraces and the bookmakers. In between the noblesse and the proletariat, in the bars, are the middle men, who may or may not have money enough for the restaurant, but who can't be bothered with the paraphernalia that goes with sitting in it. Men in the bars are semi-social about the dogs, semi-serious about it. They are having drinks, and they are having conversations, but the conversations are all about greyhounds: dog talk.

Some of those in the restaurant will be dog people, although a dog man like my father maintains that he cannot concentrate on his betting when he is having to think about food. But a lot of the people eating at greyhound stadia are simply in quest of a different type of night out. They know nothing about how to pick winners, but they like the way in which the frequent races (one every quarter-hour) punctuate their evening, and they like the tang of the atmosphere. I have taken some of them to the dogs. I am not sure how many of them ever go back again; nor indeed am I sure whether I would go myself had the dogs not been part of my life, on and off, for the last twenty years. It is an enclosed world which, unlike the world of most sports, or indeed most worlds of any kind, has not been eased open and penetrated by the powerful force of television. This means that people have to take it for what it is. They have, if they want to, to discover it for themselves. That is something we are not very used to doing nowadays; we are more accustomed to having things given to us, explained to us, lived for us; which may be why most dog people are dog people because they have been bred to be so.

But taking people to the dogs for the first time is a pleasure – to see what they make of it; to see them, usually, trying to reconcile the rather shadowless lack of self-consciousness around them with their expectations of a heightened, heavily etched other world. Almost invariably they win a great deal of money. I will intersperse the evening with explanations and hints and tips, they will smile the gracious smile of the deaf, they will select dogs that have amusing names or hilarious starting prices and I will lose on eleven out of twelve races. The only thing that I have ever been able to do for these people is to explain the racecard on which the recent form of each dog is detailed. I am about to take great pleasure in the following definitive explanation.

Below is a line from the form of Farloe Melody, the dog that won the Greyhound Derby final in 1992. It is taken from the racecard for semifinal night at Wimbledon stadium:

5	FARLOE MELODY (W)	Messrs J Davis & D Tickner	O'Donnell (Ireland)
		bd d Lodge Prince-Chini Chin Chin Au.89.Ir	

Orange 16.Jn 480 4 05.17 3343 3rd 2½ Murlens Abbey *Crowded st & 1* 28.84 +20 32.7 2/1 OR 29.24

Farloe Melody runs from trap five. The (W) means that he is considered a wide runner. Davis and Tickner are his owners, O'Donnell his trainer, and he is kennelled in Ireland. 'Bd' means that his coat is brindle. (Brindles are normally fawn, streaked with brown/black markings, but they vary a great deal in colour. Other abbreviations are 'bk' for black, 'w' for white, 'f' fawn, 'be' blue – a gorgeous slate colour*). 'D' is dog (and therefore 'b' is bitch). Lodge Prince is the dog's sire, and Chini Chin Chin his dam. (Names as bad as Chini

Chin Chin are not unusual. Providing that you stay within fifteen letters, you can call a dog whatever stupid thing you want: Lucky Boy Boy, More Salmon and Where's the Teddy are three memorably bad names. Often you are restricted by the fact that the greyhound's breeder has a prefix you must use – like Farloe, for example).

August 1989 is the dog's date, and Ireland his place, of birth, so he is, at the age of nearly three years, at his running peak. Most greyhounds start running at about eighteen or twenty months, and all are designated puppies until they reach two years. They are at their best from perhaps two and a half to three, and usually retire at just over four, although there are many, many exceptions: hurdlers and marathon runners nearly always run into their sixth year, and my father's trainer has a dog still running in graded, four-bend races at the age of nearly seven.

Farloe Melody's most recent race was on 16 June over 480 metres. He ran from trap four. His sectional time (to the winning line first time around) was 5.17 seconds, which is slow for a Derby dog, indicating that he didn't get out of the traps very well. His position from the traps was third; third also at the quarter mark; fourth at the half; third at the three-quarter mark; and his final position was third. From this we deduce that he either didn't try very hard, or that he didn't get a clear run. He finished two and a half lengths (a length being the span of a greyhound from nose to coccyx) behind Murlens Abbey, the winner of the race. But, we are told, he was crowded at the start and at the first bend, so we know that he indeed did not get a clear run (probably because of a bad trap draw and relatively slow break). The winning time of the race was 28.84 seconds; but the track was reckoned to be running twenty spots fast, so the 'real' winning time was 29.04. This again is slow – in 1989 Lodge Prince ran the course in 28.34. Farloe Melody's weight for the race was 32.7 kg, about 72 lb, which is average for a male. Dogs generally weigh somewhere between 65 and 80 lb; bitches between 55 and 70 lb. His starting price was 2/1; 'OR' stands for open race; and 29.24 was the dog's calculated time.

And there you have it. Could one extrapolate from these meagre pointers the fact that this greyhound would not just win this race, but that he would win the Derby, that no greyhound then was better than he? What mysteries are concealed within those statistics, those brief signifiers?

The Love of the Dog Man

The sport of greyhound racing is about as old as my father. It has not yet lived out a human lifespan. The dogs was born on 24 July 1926, at the Belle Vue stadium in Manchester, when the first modern greyhound race was won by Mistley, a dog with half a tail, at odds of 6/1. The dogs was the child of a union between the animal instinct to chase the scent of a hare and the human instinct to chase the scent of money: instincts which love the hope, the hunger, the helpless movement towards the elusive, the *sport*, far better than they love the attainment, the end, the acquisition of a thing that their insensate desire can only waste and destroy.

That night in Manchester saw the birth of the dogs; or, if you like, the legitimate birth, because there had been a bastard child running around since the mid-nineteenth century, especially in the north of England, a little runt born of coursing and gambling: a sport in which greyhounds, or more likely whippets, raced eagerly over waste grounds towards the deceptive fluttering of an old rag, while men betted hopefully and hopelessly on the dogs and against each other. It may have been the makeshift lure of the rag which gave to the bastard birth the name of 'flapping', which is still used to describe unlicensed greyhound tracks.

Belle Vue was built on the site of a flapping track. Men who had gambled on dogs, on boxers, on pitch-and-toss, who had been to coursing's Waterloo Cup in Liverpool, who had owned pigeons and whippets, were now compelled to try this newly formalised sport, to inhabit this stadium, this 'elaborate setting and ceremonial' (*The Sporting Chronicle*). A curiosity about how the dogs might fulfil their instinctive desires sent 1,700 of these men to the Gorton district of Manchester on that high summer evening. What must it have been like? Hats, fags, fascination. No bars, no stands, no comfort. Five races of seven dogs apiece, a hurdle race for six dogs. Coursing greyhounds, many of them owned by the aristocracy, who, in letting their dogs try something new and amusing, were thus laying the foundations for a great working man's sport. Bookmakers, absolutely unaware of how to work out the odds. Who were these dogs? Their abilities were a mystery. Mistley was 6/1 and he won his race by eight lengths – he should have been 6/1 *on*, for God's sake. No previous form, no tasty little bits of inside information to go on – all night the bookmakers must have been chalking up prices with tremulously daring hands, nerves a-crackle, thrilling and singing to an unknown tune. Of course the punters didn't know much either, but their nerves, too, must have been twitching with this new blend of sensations: the tang of glamour upon the familiar raw tastes; the sense of occasion that was weighting and ritualising the instinctive desire to chase money. Beyond and within that elusive scent, did the men sense a steadier promise, the hope of a lasting love affair with the dogs, the sport that they had perhaps been waiting for? That night in Manchester, the legitimate child of the formal union between animal and human instinct was blessed with a christening. Now the dogs was off.

1926 was the year of the General Strike. In such hard times for the working class, the dogs was welcomed like a lover by anyone who thrilled to the feel of speed and the lure of money; like a gloriously fascinating lover, one who gives and takes away, who fulfils and frustrates, who insinuates and infuses itself into the lives of those that love. You worked long hours, your wages were subsistence merely, you had to gamble with street bookmakers, or on whippets running after a bit of rag, or on an annual visit to Aintree; you had little to fill your limited hours of freedom except football or snooker or some shadowy silent film . . . and suddenly, here was this thing, all ready for you, every night if you wanted it, welcoming you with its visceral thrills and its elusive promises! The dogs sang its siren song to the working man and helplessly he listened. By 31 July 1926, the crowd at Belle Vue had gone up to 16,000. By 1927, attendances for the licensed tracks were just over 5½ million. By 1928, they were well over 13½ million. By 1945 they were easily 50 million, and however many of these attendances were the same obsessives going over and over again, that is still a great many people in love – or at the very least loosely infatuated – with the dogs.

In its youth the sport was made mighty and confident by the simplicity with which it exerted its power. It spread and it bloomed, intertwining itself with the lives of millions, like a tree growing into the house alongside it. Its coursing roots were old, as old as the relationship between men and animals, as old as the countryside, and its gambling roots stretched down into an unfathomable past: so how could its newness fail to delight? Also, as with football, it seemed to need you. It *did* need you. It needed and was needed, like all true sport. On the night of the Greyhound Derby at White City stadium in 1946, there were forty-four other race meetings taking place around Britain. On that night, nearly 2,500 dogs cracked out their half-minute runs; the traps whiplashed open nearly 400 times; more than 250,000 people staked more than £1 million in bets; more than 50,000 of those people bonded together in a sensual moment which peaked and evanesced even as Monday's News crossed the winning line in the fastest Derby that had yet been run; and, after six years of blackouts, of shadowless afternoon meetings, the lights streamed through the teeming oval arena of White City stadium, people saw and felt the play of brilliance upon night, saw and felt that they were gloriously, gaudily, grittily alive – on that night, that early summer night in 1946, greyhound racing was at its height, it was a colossus of a sport.

But the end of the war turned the lights on in people's lives as well, and possibilities, hitherto only glimpsed in dreams, presented themselves and demanded to be grasped. The working man had won a war, he had been given hopes of material rewards, of solid prizes that he would not have to gamble in order to win – how could he ever need greyhound racing in quite the same way again? Love does not always disappear in the face of other loves, but the quality of that love almost always changes.

People did not stop loving the dogs – it is still, after

that other great love, football, the most popular spectator sport in Britain – but it no longer weaved its way so easily through the lives of the masses. The attendances of 1945 had halved by 1948. A fuel crisis caused all tracks to close for six weeks from 1947 to 1948 and limited racing until 1949, which contributed to the decline; but ten years earlier the habit of the dogs would not have been lost so readily. The heavy betting taxes imposed by the Government soured the bitter-sweet pleasure of gambling, but people were willing to pay even higher levies in betting shops. The opening of betting shops in 1961 is usually blamed for luring people away from the dogs, but by 1960 attendances had already fallen to just over 15 million. Now they are just over 4 million. In 1945 there were seventy-seven registered tracks. Now there are thirty-seven. In 1946 more than 50,000 people went to the Derby final. In 1993, fewer than 8,000 bothered to go.

In the days of its prime, greyhound racing seemed infinitely generative of its power, but as it grew older life left it behind, perhaps because the way in which people connect with the world around them has changed during the 66 years of the dogs. People now do not seem to *need* to connect with the world. Their relationship with it is both more and less sophisticated. They know more about the world but perhaps understand less. They demand more but give and receive less. Television has a lot to do with this and is probably the real reason for the decline of the dogs: it is the most powerful love of all, because it can be an alternative to anything. It can reshape the world and render it unsatisfactory, disappointing, difficult, not worth the trouble. Some people seem now to go greyhound racing in search of a screen world, a black and white world of Rank Organisation spivs or a prawn cocktail colour world of media-mythical Essex men. From occupying a proud, even necessary place in sporting culture, the dogs now keeps a dimly picturesque corner in popular social history: a thing that people have never not known about but have never really known about, a thing that, as with many old things, is loved not with a passion but with indulgence.

Except, of course, that there are still what one might call dog people. On Monday night at Catford, on Thursday night at Milton Keynes, on Saturday morning at Hackney, if the dog people know of a good thing, a sure thing, a class greyhound, then they'll be there having a look, having a proper bet, creating atmosphere by their absolute indifference to doing so. There were once millions of dog people. Now there are tens of thousands. Like my father, they grew up with the sport, or their fathers grew up with the sport; it has always simply intertwined with their lives. Those who take out an image of the dogs from their current account with the Media Bank have nothing to do with the dog people. Dog people are absolutely what they are, doing absolutely the thing they want to be doing, casually and unthinkingly in love with the dogs.

In the mid-1980s, greyhound racing was a dwarf of a sport. The Greyhound Racing Association (GRA), the limited company which had been born with the dogs in 1926 and which owned most of the major stadia, had diversified and invested in property with a ruinous mixture of abandon and ignorance. The land on which the

stadia stood was worth far more by now than the tracks
could possibly generate, and the GRA was forced to sell
off several of its assets in order to pay its huge debts,
White City – perhaps the most famous of all greyhound
tracks – among them. The loss of this elegant white
stadium, quite different from all others and secretly acknowledged by them as their lord and master, symbolised
not only the severance of the most important link with
the past, but also the destruction of a touchstone, a
standard against which the dogs could measure itself:
even though it usually didn't. On that autumn day in
1984 when White City crumbled into a pile of nothing-
ness upon a vast wasteland in Shepherd's Bush – the
sort of land on which, 100 years earlier, wraith-like
whippets had begun to conjure an image of the dogs –
greyhound racing reached its lowest point, for it now
knew that the only way that it could live was by killing
the best things about itself.

Hard times for people meant easy times for the dogs,
and easy times for people have meant hard times for the
dogs. Since the war, the more enterprising tracks have
tried to resolve this paradox by making the dogs part of
the easy life. Forty years ago this meant building a
restaurant and a few bars; today it means remaking the
stadia in the late twentieth century image of Leisuretown. Clean and ghastly and strung about with
televisions to watch the race that one can't quite be
bothered to look at while it is actually happening, these
terrible sports centres are attracting corporate hospitality, couples having a night out, syndicates of people
getting together to buy a greyhound and so on and so
forth. The dog people take no notice. As the pine fittings

and taupe furnishings move in around them, they keep their heads down and study the form. They are the heart of the dogs; but most sports survive today by pandering to those who loudly profess their allegiance, rather than those who silently swear it.

Greyhound racing is still in all sorts of financial trouble. Unlike horse racing, it gets no levy from the bookmakers in the form of a percentage of all bets wagered, and now it must grapple with the consequences of the Government's 1993 decision to allow summer (April to August) evening opening of betting shops. This, say the tracks, will lose them at least 10 per cent of their custom and thus render them uneconomic. The solution to these problems, it would seem, is for the dogs to deny its lary* old heart and become an upright citizen of Leisuretown. Yet it is the love of sport that keeps sport going, market it how you will.

My father is a dog person. He is of an age with the dogs; they literally grew up together. I am not a dog person but I was a dog child, an owner at the age of nine. Men of the world keep in with other men of the world by little favours, and my father's breeder saw that the simplest token of all would be to indulge this child with the gift of a white-and-blue puppy called London Lights. He was born in 1973, so is long dead, though I knew nothing of his life after he stopped racing. One rarely does with greyhounds. I can recall standing on the broad and sloping steps at Harringay* on a light summer evening, down by the bookmakers, surrounded by dog men and watching London Lights win the first race at about 4/1. Aping the men, as children will, I tried to conceal my excitement with nonchalance, but I couldn't get over the fact that *my* dog, *my* baby, had proved himself in this adult world. I had seen him rolling on his back in his kennel and leaping towards my hand as I said my unbearable goodbye; now here he was at work, causing these men to win or lose real money.

Dog children are quite common. They like the greyhounds and they like the finite statistics of the racecards. I used to compile these, so familiar was I with the complement of dogs at White City and Harringay, and can remember my father muttering: 'That's not a bad race', when I presented him with one. A certain type of child is fascinated by the minutiae that goes into making up a race: the one dog gets out of the trap but the three dog is fast up to the first bend and likes to get to the rails so might knock the one and two out of it which could leave the four clear but the six finishes strongest of the lot of them but the five dog is the class dog. The boy inside a racing manager is perhaps also reassured by these pure statistics, so far removed from the troubling minutiae that he must deal with in his man's world: how to keep aware of the tricks that might be played by certain trainers, how to keep certain owners happy, how to keep the punters happy, how to give them the occasional sure thing.

Not only did I compile racecards but, in my unquestioning love for the dogs, I began a novel, influenced heavily by *Watership Down*, in which the narrator was a greyhound. I took him from birth in Ireland, through irresponsible puppyhood, through the death of his sister, through to the beginnings of his working life, at which point the facts became too slippery and adult for me to shape. I also wrote school essays about greyhound racing. Mine was a stage school, and if its pupils were asked to imagine what they would like to be when they grew up, the acceptable answer was a ballerina, a musical star, even a Bluebell Girl; I, however, wrote that I wished to grow up to be a greyhound trainer. My mother was aghast. Her impeccable appearance at open days was, she believed, being penetrated as a disguise; the assembled staff was collectively disrobing her of her Sonia Rykiel suit and dressing her in the Persian cat sweater and white cowboy boots that she was surely going to change into as soon as she attained her blanc-mange boudoir. And all those concerned, ladylike inquiries into her daughter's progress at the piano ... nobody was fooled. They knew that she was yearning to tip them the wink about the dead cert running at Hackney Wick that afternoon, yearning indeed to be down there herself, eating jellied eels with the Pearly King. Even people such as my mother, who like dog racing, can be embarrassed about admitting to liking it. They know what it is really like, the subtler realities within the perceived image of the Rank Organisation spiv and the Essex Man, but they also know what people think it is like. (In fact, my mother's concern was not entirely misplaced. The daughter of the big bookmaker, Bernard Coral, was also at my school, and the periodic sweep up the drive of his bright gold Rolls-Royce was always met with that English display of amused, disgusted snobbishness which masks a faintly panic-stricken envy. No such concealment of feelings at the dogs, where if you had a bloody great Roller you bloody well flashed around in it. As you cruised like a king into the carpark at The Stow*, taking ten minutes to reverse into a space, you took as your due the admiring grins and sneers of openly jealous men, men who viewed a Rolls-Royce in much the same way as the aspiring aristocracy view entry to the Royal Enclosure at Ascot: as a totemic validation of their lives.)

At the Hook Kennels every Sunday there were plenty of flash cars belonging to rich owners. I would be taken there in one myself, protected from the adult realities of how cars and greyhounds were paid for; while my father talked dog talk, I was with the dogs. Hook Kennels had been built in Northaw, Hertfordshire, on land bought by the GRA in the early 1930s for the purpose of housing dogs that ran at its London tracks. It was, in its way, a rather beautiful place, of sloping lanes fringed with clumps of cottages and boxes of kennels, of airy masses of foliage, of inconceivable acres of fields with, rising discreetly at the centre, a rather grand white house in which lived, in fine hierarchical fashion, the kennels' general manager. The trainers and their staff lived in the cottages. One of my father's trainers lived in a barren lodge, very close to the local lunatic asylum. As if he didn't have enough dogs to deal with, the trainer had one of his own, a timorous, voluminous Alsatian called Satan. Was Satan there as protection against the next-door neighbours? He can hardly have been there to protect the lodge, which was bereft of any feature that might have interested a burglar. It was, in fact, bereft of almost any essential feature; although the trainer did very well without a kettle, for example, by heating mugs of coffee in the oven.

Having originally been a country estate, the Hook Kennels were beautiful and natural in their form, but the content of this form was fairly rough and ready.

Nowadays it would all be tarted up, Barratt homes for the trainers and virulent brick pizza huts for the dogs, but laid out in some inexplicably flat and ugly way, with rows of garden-city trees against which the greyhounds would hardly dare to stop. Except that nothing like it would exist any more. Today, the white house is inhabited by a Maharishi-type guru and his followers. The GRA, forced by debt to cede ever more jewels in its crown throughout the 1970s and 1980s, culminating in the sale of White City, gradually sold off the valuable Hook land. Trainers today all have their own kennel establishments. This is better in some ways – it must have been somewhat peculiar for grown men to be living under the blatant patronage of the GRA – but although people always think that they want the responsibility that comes with independence, they sometimes actually don't. Training kennels today are just as rough and ready as the Hook, and just as well run, but they lack the form, the order, that comes from being sheltered by the past and by benignly stern authority. Maybe it is that I have a child's understanding of the place – although I think that children can feel perfectly well the difference between a regulated establishment and a chaotic establishment, and these kennels felt regulated to me; perhaps because their beginnings came from the days when greyhound racing reigned strong and adored and indifferent to rivals.

The smell of dusty fur, of cracked leather leads, of brown bread soaking in tin sinks, of rusty water filmed with a skin of hairs and saliva, of dog mouths drooling and snapping for clammy worms of minced meat and moist dark leaves of cabbage, of dog piss streaming its rivulets away from every tree; a smell which, within the dim corridors of the kennels, clung tight to each nostril hair, and which carried out its memory even into the high pure air of the stretching fields; a smell which, when my brain illuminates its store of slides, I can now almost conjure back into my nose: except that the slides are partly destroyed, the clear pictures fading into shapes of half-rooms and outlines of half-buildings, both fraying into mistiness, into textures of walls, into qualities of light, into the way that a landmark, a person or a dog engaged with my eyes.

We had an angel dog at home but I yearned for those greyhounds. There was pride and reflected glory in walking them – I knew how successful some of them were and knew dimly that they were objects of envy – although there was always the fear of treading on their paws; always when they walked beside me I could imagine those delicately bunched, costly little feet flattening and splaying beneath my lumbering shoe. The fear was doubled because I knew that these were not just my dogs. They also belonged to a world beyond me. When they leapt hungrily towards me through the bars of their kennels, their sloping eyes avid for attention and their muzzles slack around eager tongues, what enthralled me was the containment of this ordinariness, this greed for food and fuss, this dog-likeness, within these overbred, purposeful, incongruously beautiful frames. These dogs were like a phalanx of fabulous catwalk models gathered into a downmarket pub, roaring over packets of crisps and – as girls will – wanting to catch the eyes of men who were less glorious than they, but not therefore more human. So these were my dogs, and I loved them as dogs, but I somehow felt privileged to be able to do so.

As the world of the dogs spreads out from the central point which is the dogs themselves, so too did the Hook Kennels. The social life of greyhound racing, of which I then understood nothing, was, of course, existing side by side with all the dog visiting and dog walking, but I didn't realise that. I thought we were all there purely to confirm our love affair with these greyhounds. The social bit I thought was tacked on afterwards so as not to be too early for Sunday lunch. To me, it had nothing to do with the dogs. In fact, although I can't remember a single word that was uttered in the dreadful bar into which everybody shoved themselves at about 12.30, it must all have been dog talk. 'That dog of his is a bit special. That had been laid off for weeks and that was twenty spots off the track record in a trial at Wembley, and they don't go well first time round Wembley as a rule. That little bitch of mine, that little brindle, she was top grade at White City and I gave her a trial round Wembley and she – well, she graded, nothing special though, if you understand me. But that big dog, that ran in the heats of that open on Friday – and that *walked* out of the traps – ! I thought, Christ, I've done my money here – cos I got 3/1 on him, and that was a little bit of value – got murdered at the first bend – bugger, he must have been six lengths behind that bitch that was second to the Derby winner a couple of weeks ago, so *she* can run a bit, make no mistake. Then I tell you what, that dog, that slooshed up the back straight like all the other buggers was standing still. Won it by two lengths. And he got *murdered* at the first bend. I tell you what, if he

39

could trap, that really would be some sort of greyhound. But he don't always trap. He's unreliable. But he's a beautiful looking dog. Looks like his father.'

Dog talk. I love dog talk now – makes me feel *really* grown up – but when I think about that bar all I can remember is the pain of true boredom. Cut off from my dogs, cut off from my father, who was at the base of a spiral of dog talk, terrified of the loping, sullen kennel boys who played billiards and put Deep Purple on a jukebox whose noise was smothered beneath the rising layers of dog talk, overcome by the acrid smell of Watney's beer which spilled on to the floor in careless pools, like the dog piss in the kennels; all I could do was retire to a room with closed curtains and a television, watch *Thunderbirds* and eat Golden Wonder crisps. Occasionally other dog children would come in. I don't remember liking any of them particularly, it was the dogs that I liked, and probably I wanted to be the only dog child around. I did start showing off about one of our dogs to a little girl who then silenced me as effectively as the arrival of a Chanel-suited beauty will silence a gaggle of giggling women: her parents had owned Patricia's Hope, the dog that had won four Derbys – the Scottish, the Welsh, and the English, twice. He could trap all right.

This dog child was especially galling to me because Patricia's Hope had his name up – twice – on the board which listed all Hook-trained winners of English classic races. This board was the only thing about the bar which I liked. I studied it every Sunday, willing my father's name on to it, but although he had won many top races with his dogs, he has never won a classic.

Children often love to play at what they perceive to be

the organised world of adulthood. As well as compiling racecards, I used to love keeping a ledger of our greyhounds, listing in my careful writing (a crossing-out would have ruined the whole fancy) whatever prize money they had earned against their kennel fees. Recently I found one of these ledgers. I hadn't realised that we had had so many of these dogs, indeed so many – about ten runners every week – that I couldn't remember some of them *at all*. The name London Lights recurred, sometimes with a red pen beside his name to denote a win (he won a lot of races – was the sort of dog, in fact, that I should be delighted to own now). Pitman's Brief, Chain Gang – I remember them perfectly, black brother and sister, smooth, sleek and charged-looking, successful open racers. I remember Sun Chariot for his beautiful face – pale fawn, and the black eyes fringed with a yearning outline, like those of an Italian starlet receiving Holy Communion – and for the evening when I fell asleep on the sofa waiting for my father to return from seeing him run in an open race, and awoke to see a dim figure sloping gleefully into the living-room, clutching a silver trophy. Towards the end of the year, my entries in the ledger book stop. They continue for a few pages in the adult hand of my father, then those too stop, since presumably the ledger book had been kept up only to amuse me.

It had been just before that time that a puzzling and frightening shadow had fallen across the ever-open door that led my father and I on to the dogs. His enthusiasm for his sport had become dimmed and forced. There were occasional phone calls, during which the conversation would scuffle and halt and it would become suddenly necessary discreetly to close a door. Once I picked up the extension and heard the words, '. . . I'm so sorry about . . .', at which point I put the phone down, not wanting to know anything. I didn't want to know about my mother's red eyes. I preferred to believe her when she cursed the onions, or laughed that she needed Optrex. I didn't want to hear the sad, stiff undertone to my father's jaunty replies to my questions about the dogs.

It was one dog only, the death of one dog only, but he had been perhaps our best and, not entirely coincidentally, our favourite. Commutering was a big, brindle dog, a very male-looking dog, with ears that liked to prick themselves into tall triangles. He won many open races. Our house is full of his beautiful prizes. We keep bottles in wine-coolers won by him, serve the wine in glasses won by him, placed on trays won by him. In 1970 he broke the track record at the long-closed, pre-metric West Ham stadium, so he will always be the fastest dog in the world over 700 yards. He was loved for the fact that he was one of the few greyhounds – 'They're the stupid ones, really', my father would say – that will always give their all to a race and run it from the heart. He looked as he ran: very fine, very gentlemanly, class and dependability both beyond question, a Bentley of a dog.

One of the pleasures of my life then was to run a slow, firm hand down the thin tiger stripes of his long back and to see the streaks appearing one by one, tight, groomed, alert and shimmering with bone. He welcomed one wildly at the kennels, thrusting towards one with his head flat and his mouth agape, like a dragon.

His reputation was considerable and, in the way of some sportsmen, women, animals, he was always regarded with admiring respect, so one was all the more intoxicated by his nature, which was loyal, warm, stalwart, and speckled with silliness. He was the sort of dog that makes me feel that he would know me still if he were alive today.

I feel now that he forged a partnership with my father, whom I can still see casually fondling the sensitive brindle ears. They understood one another. Throughout his life, Commutering did the right thing by my father: he tried and he won and he loved.

He went to stud and threw some good dogs in the short time before he got cancer. That was what all the phone calls were about. Normally that sort of sympathy would not be extended for the loss of a racing greyhound, but real dog people love their dogs and they were sorry for my parents, who were deemed to have lost their boy. Much later, some time after the confusion of my intimations had been straightened, even relieved, by the sad and simple facts, I learned that Commutering could have been saved had the vet been allowed to amputate one of his legs. 'Oh . . .!' I had said, thinking hard, so hard, so taken with this information, which seemed somehow to present an escape from finality, that I felt for a moment that the dog was still alive and the decision still to be made. My father was walking away from me towards his chair and preparing to sit after a day's work. 'I wasn't going to do that to the old feller', he said as he sat and unfolded his newspaper, and I understood that he had done the right thing by his racing greyhound in allowing him to die calm and intact.

But with Commutering died the child's view of the dogs, the fairytale of the eternal present in which the same, beautiful, beloved animals lived for ever. When London Lights suddenly 'retired' I didn't dare ask what had happened to him. I just forgot him. I remember him now, walking beside me as I looked down upon the long, bunched swoop of back, the ribs that wobbled gently from side to side in time with the obedient trot. At the time I had no thought but that I would always be taking those walks.

But the death of Commutering was succeeded by the birth of my adolescence, and it was easier to forget, throwing myself as I was into myself rather than into the dogs. The familiar stadia of White City and Harringay, for which I had once been an aspiring trainer, or racing manager, became places to have a night out and stare at boys. The Derby finals were still occasions, but I *knew* they were occasions. I spent most of my evenings at the dogs looking at myself in the Ladies' mirror and wondering why people were wearing such unbelievable clothes and how they could be so unquestioningly interested in this thing. I hardly noticed when White City became debris and Harringay became Sainsbury's. When I thought about it, I thought it was a shame and a waste; but I hardly thought about it. The dog child had not become a dog person.

And I believed that coming back to greyhound racing after fifteen years was not going to make me a dog person. I felt that the dogs and I would be gruff and cheery friends, not lovers. Just as I might look at a couple who glare fondly and dribble remarks *sotto voce* at one another in a restaurant, and think, how the hell do they sustain their interest beyond this one exhausting evening's interchange; so I would think, yes, I understand a fortnightly greyhound meeting, a daily skirting accumulation of the front page of *The Greyhound Life*, lovely, delightful, the brisk thrill of feeling the blood trundle quick and ordinary – but *every* meeting, *every* word, *every* opinion, a sentence without remission and without the desire for remission? How could I do that? How do dog people do it?

The life of the dog person is bound to his sport by either, or both, of two extraordinarily strong ties. There is the tie of ownership, which binds the dog person to the fate of his greyhound, and there is the tie of gambling, which binds him to fate itself. Once submitted to, the power of either, or both, of these is almost inescapable, for they continually create, fulfil and thwart desire. They are as unpredictable as life; they *are* life; yet they are controlled and distanced, because they live within the world of sport, whose rhythms are repetitive, seasonal, reassuring, predictable. This is the dialectic at the heart of sport, that it is the unpredictable within the predictable. Its structure is a regulation of life, yet, within that structure, ungovernable life is happening.

It didn't take very long for one of the ties that bind to furl itself around my heart and attach me again to the dogs. Gambling could never become an intrinsic part of my life; that is not my nature; but as soon as I began again to visit greyhounds in their kennels, to watch them run, to read about their runs in *The Greyhound Life*, to ring up my father to find out how they had trialled, to have a small bet on one of them, which meant having to get *The Greyhound Life* the next day to find out how they got on and then having to visit the kennels to reward them and then having to go to the next meeting and see them run again – and perhaps have another small bet on perhaps that other dog that I walked last Sunday and then . . . this is how it happens. This is how it becomes inescapable. This is how the repetitiveness of sport becomes another tie that binds itself to one's life; how, indeed, it becomes inseparable from one's life.

This doesn't quite mean that I have become a dog person. My concentration on the dogs is too fanciful. I know, in truth, that what is deep at the heart of my love for it is the child's view of the dogs, which has been re-discovered in writing this book. Greyhound racing has become to me now a symbol of the connection between my childhood and adulthood; a connection which, as an adolescent, I would have disdained, but which now, at twenty-eight, and at the onset of the years in which the fact of adulthood becomes inescapable, engages me very strongly.

Of course greyhound racing would never be a con-scious symbol of anything to the true dog person. Symbols imply retrospection, and he inhabits the moment by moment present of his sport. Anything that takes him from that, any decorative attitudinising, is an irrelevance. His memories are stored and cherished like claret in a cellar; his expectations are boundless as a child's; but past and future never really deflect his atten-tion from the present. It is *today*'s *Greyhound Life* that he is reading as if it were *The Story of O*. It is photographs of *this* litter in Ireland that he is studying with a metaphor-ical spyglass to detect the pure lines of breeding within the fuzz of puppyishness. It is *tonight*'s racecard that he is teasing out, like a woman unpicking a rogue seam, with the trainer whose phone call he has awaited as if from – yes, a lover. The repetitive details accumulate like the tiny moments which have gone to create a life, a life which is even now being lived.

And so, reading old copies of *The Greyhound Magazine**, reading every day *The Greyhound Life*, talking to men like my father, I observed the process of the accumulation of details that make up the parallel life, the eyes-down pursuance of its magnetic thread. I know that what I had loved most about the child's view of the dogs was the absorption of it, the pure, unwitting concentration upon the here and now. Adult concentration I have always believed to be a tatty, to-and-fro thing – eyes always flickering round the fragmenting fluxive paths of life, mind ever-familiar with the idea of alternative routes, of fogginess, of deviations, of roadworks, of mapless territories – yet here, rediscovering the dogs, I was brought face to face again with the child's concentration, and it was buried deep within the heads of men.

The true lover of sport loves innocently, conceal this how he will. That is why, after only a short time of researching this book, I was flooded with a sudden and momentarily unbearable perception of pathos. A piece of paper given to my father from Oxford Stadium, decorated with drawings of greyhounds, proclaiming in huge letters: 'Fastest 450m Grader of the Week – Jerpoint Ali – 27.46'. An advertisement in the Irish newspaper *The Sporting Press*, purporting to have been inserted by the stud dog One to Note: 'Congratulations to my son Lartigue Note on winning the 1989 English Derby'. *The Greyhound Magazine*: page after page of filigree-detailed minutiae, of passionate opinions barely

clothed in the adult robes of irony and restraint. Tight
rage at the attitude of the Government which briefly
banned the dogs during the oil crisis of the mid-1970s:
'Why do they always pick on greyhound racing . . . It
really ought to have its own Greyhound Race Relations
Act to protect it.' Twee admiration of former champions: '. . . a dusky maiden called Dolores Rocket hit the
scene in 1971 and provided thousands of racegoers, including yours truly, with their most memorable Derby'.
A crossword: 'What was the name of the dog that won
the first race ever run in 1926?' A quiz: 'How many
words can you find in the word G R E Y H O U N D?'
Pictures of dead dogs, 'At Stud, Camira Story, one of
the world's fastest greyhounds', caught perfectly alert to
the alien click of the camera, standing upon their casual
sturdy pride, young and male, bristling with the brief
touch of a celebrity that these photographs have no
thought will ever come to an end. The eternal present
within the eternal progress that is sport . . .

An article about Commutering and his brother After
the Show, who had liked my father so much that when
he returned him to his kennel he would bite hold of his
tie to stop him leaving. 'Yeah, well, he was a bloody
nuisance . . . Let's have a look at that', said my father,
indicating the fifteen-year-old magazine. He pretended
to be scanning the article but it was obvious that he was
reading it intensely. 'There was a time when the presence of Commutering in the field was frightening off
the opposition. All flesh is mortal, however, and the
mighty Commutering was somehow to be denied a classic success . . . before he decided to hang up his racing
jacket Commutering had won forty-seven NGRC opens

. . . After the Show could well have topped his brother's impressive total of wins had not injury cut short his career.' There was a picture of After the Show, running for the line, limbs collected together, tail swishing low and heavy as a crocodile's, in his eye the lawless gleam of absolute determination; and one of Commutering, his ears in their tall triangles, possibly my hand on the lead against which he is minimally straining, some unknown stimulus having aroused his willing instincts.

A dual intensity was being given to the article, that of pride remembered and that of pride re-experienced. 'You can have this back,' my father said to me, waving it nonchalantly, 'but I'll just take it down the kennels tomorrow.' He wanted to show it to his trainer and to Roy, the man with whom he has owned dogs for the last few years. It was the present that he cared about, but this article was not just about past dogs, past sport, it was his own past, a past which has been twinned with greyhound racing, and sometimes moments from the past fill one's body as if the whole of it is breathing, as if the present has never become the past.

3

Beginnings

It was Mick the Miller, the most famous dog that has ever, will ever, run, bursting upon greyhound racing when it was only three years old, who was magnificently and eternally to justify the dog man's love for his sport. Mick the Miller's three-year reign, from 1929 to 1931, during which time he won five classic races and broke four world records, made him a sporting and working-class hero. In an age before television and newspaper became creators of celebrity, Mick the Miller created his own, without hype, without help, without precedent. Greyhound racing did not know that it could create such a powerful phenomenon, that a greyhound could be loved and worshipped in the way that this one would be; the sport had not been searching for Mick the Miller, he took it completely by surprise. He could not have *made* people love the dogs, but he reassured them that they were right to love it. Look, he said to them, this is what it can be like. Have faith. This thing isn't just a maddening and repetitive love affair from which you cannot ex-tricate yourselves, however much you might sometimes wish to. There is magic here too, magic and the stuff of myth.

After that first night in Belle Vue, many bold men –

promoters, owners and trainers – had thrown themselves at the dogs as if into a fire from which they prayed
– *believed* – a phoenix would rise. They had seen that it
had only taken a week in the life of greyhound racing for
its followers to grow by 1,000 per cent; but still they were
courageous, because it could have been just a trend, and
buying land, creating a stadium and persuading people
to race dogs inside it require more energy and invest-
ment than are merited by a passing fancy. Obviously the
promoters nurtured the dog man's love for his new
sport. They made it so important and omnipresent that
he had little chance of escaping; but eventually, had he
wanted to escape, he would have done so. If he had
merely had a crush on the dogs, he would have got over
it and gone back to – well, what? This was the root of the
matter. What could he go back to? What could he find in
his world that would fulfil and frustrate those desires
within him that the dogs fulfilled and frustrated?

Greyhound racing was his love and he didn't *want* to
get over it. He wanted to stay with it. This was *his* sport,
wonderful bastard thing, *his* love, gorgeous bloody cow,
and it always left him wanting more of it because every
time he encountered it he failed to suss it, failed to beat
it, failed to convince himself that it really did love him in
return.

So I don't believe that, had there been no Mick the
Miller, greyhound racing would have failed to grow
beyond the shooting spurts of its early years. However
fascinating a creature this dog was, his influence would
have disappeared with him, had dog men not truly loved
the dogs. Of course Mick must have attracted people
who then lost interest when they realised that greyhound

racing was not full of dogs like him, just as England win-ning the World Cup interested people in football who then made their excuses to it when they discovered how unbearably boring it could be. But to a real dog man, or a real football lover, sublime successes like Mick the Miller or Bobby Charlton cannot make them worship their sport any more than they do already. The sport is the vessel which contains within it the sublime suc-cesses, and indeed the abysmal failures; and the vessel is the thing that they love.

But the sublime successes justify the love. It's all worthwhile, they seem to say. Stick with it and you will have moments like these. And for a dog like Mick the Miller to have appeared so early in the history of his sport, when expectations were still so beautifully new and high – how clearly he must have told all those who had created that initial explosion of faith they they had been right to do so, that greyhound racing could pro-duce stars of such brilliance that millions and millions of people would want to follow their course.

All the promoters must have wanted to kiss the dog's peerless little cat feet. With hindsight one can say that greyhound racing would have thrived with or without him, but at the time it must have seemed as though the phoenix arising from the fire into which the promoters had thrown themselves was, indeed, Mick the Miller – and the *memory* of Mick the Miller. After he had gone, his myth would still be there. Just as dog men return over and over to the dogs to see if *this* will be the time that they conquer it, so now they were enthralled by the idea that the sport might, at any time, produce another hero for them. All the new owners, all the new trainers, all the new tracks that had stood up and declared themselves during the last years of the 1920s (White City, Harringay, Wembley, West Ham, Clapton, Wimbledon in London, Hall Green and Perry Barr in Birmingham, Brough Park in Newcastle, Monmore in Wolverhampton, Henlow in Bedfordshire, Slough, Brighton, Ramsgate, Middlesbrough, Hull, White City in Cardiff, Powderhall in Edinburgh, Shelbourne and Harold's Cross in Dublin, Celtic Park and Dunmore Park in Belfast – and many, many more) had always known that every single race they created gave birth, however momentarily, to a hope. Now every single greyhound would do the same thing. The sport of dog men – that amorphous, anonymous lover – had been given by Mick the Miller a proud identity, a name, a face.

Again, with hindsight, it is easy to see that greyhound racing was bound to be popular, because those stadia were competing with nothing for the patronage of the dog men. Still, the speed of growth is amazing when one really thinks about it. How often are ideas so quickly accepted and acted upon? Shilling shares in the GRA up to £37 10s. after the first three months of the sport. Attendances up to 17 million by 1930. 220 tracks – most of them flappers – by 1932. So much hope being thrown into the fire – it was as if a touchpaper had been lit and thrown upon the most inflammable ground, as eager and arid as tinder. Of course the world had been readying itself for the dogs since long before 1926; the sport had, in fact, been gestating for exactly fifty years. The first ever greyhound race had been run in 1876 at a sporting ground in Hendon, north London, called the Welsh Harp. Newspaper reports of this event make it sound marginal, a one-off, a quirky little story of the kind that might now swell a regional news programme; it is extraordinary to realise that in it lay the template for a sport that would hold millions of people in its thrall. A stuffed hare, hand-powered by a winch and pursued by just two dogs, wobbled 400 yards down a straight course and then disappeared under a snuff, not to emerge again for half a century. No drama, no surprise, no sport. The headline under which the race was covered in *The Times* was 'Coursing by Proxy', and that is exactly what it was, except that the unpredictable element in coursing, which derives from the fact that one doesn't know what the hare is going to do, had not been replaced by the unpredictable element in racing, which derives from the fact that the track is too tightly-shaped for the number of dogs running around it. The Welsh Harp race had nothing, really, to do with greyhound racing. But it did differ vitally from coursing, and not just because of the stuffed hare. It was the first modern greyhound race because this was the first time that the dogs had been raced in a formal setting – and, more importantly, in an *urban* setting. It proved that a transition might be possible from the natural, country pursuit of coursing to the organised, citified sport of racing.

Sport is frivolous fighting. It is the regulation and etiolation of the essential warrior skill. All sports contain within them the origin of necessity and, usually, the better the sport the more apparent its origin. It is the origin of necessity which gives to sport that quality of *panic* which makes it exciting to watch: something more primitive than the desire to win a game is spiking the adrenalin of those that play. Running, chasing, eluding, jumping, aiming, throwing, catching – always within the demonstration of these skills is the shadow of hunger, of need, of escape from pursuit. Men still carry a rugby ball as if it were a baby that they had just rescued from the jaws of a sabre-toothed tiger. Greyhounds still run after a mechanical hare as if they might catch it and kill it, for dog racing developed from coursing, and coursing was a necessity which became a blood sport which became a gambler's sport – same animal instinct, different human instincts.

To watch a greyhound chase a hare which had to be caught, for food, would be an extraordinary thrill, edges of fire around desperation. To watch a greyhound chase a hare which need nor need not be caught, for sport, would be another kind of thrill, edges of fire around fear and desire. To watch a greyhound chase a hare which can never be caught is another kind of thrill – the subject of this book – an owner's thrill, a gambler's thrill, but one which, however distanced it becomes from its origin of necessity, contains within it still the memory of coursing, the ghosts of its reality, the kernel of panic.

But from these identical seeds have grown two very dissimilar bodies. Put crudely, it is as if a pair of twins had been separated at birth, one of them to be raised by an English country gentleman, the other by a self-made millionaire living in a large city. The worlds of coursing and of racing could hardly be more different. Of course, there is a crossover between the two, because some coursing men like the dogs and some dog men like coursing. Many dog men make an annual, and literal, crossover to Ireland each February to attend a big coursing meeting at Clonmel, in Tipperary; once there, subsumed into that larger and more unified dog world, they visit their breeders, look at their new pups, listen to the dog talk, suss out what's going to be this year's Irish hot shot ('Broke twenty-nine round Shelbourne? Did it, b'Christ?'), plan to come back to England and have a nice antepost bet on it before the Derby, drink pints of Jamesons and go without sleep for seventy-two hours. In Ireland, where horses, dogs and gambling form a trium- virate as capable of uniting all classes of men as the Father, the Son and the Holy Ghost, the world of cours- ing is very close in spirit to that of track racing. Coursing in Ireland is simply a rural variation of the dogs; it has a similar hierarchy of races; it even has a Derby, just as prestigious as the Irish track Derby. The hares are of as little importance as they are in racing. There simply as a means of starting the race, they are bred to get away as quickly as possible; they are the size of small dogs and they are very rarely killed. They are necessary, but irre- levant. They are not equal players in the spectacle with the greyhounds, because coursing in Ireland is not a blood sport; it is, like racing, a betting sport.

But coursing in England, open field coursing, is not in its heart a betting sport. Its world is that of the English country gentleman; and he is rarely a gambling man, because gambling, however foolish it may be, has a point to it, and the English country gentleman prefers to do things that have no point. The English race as a whole loves the apparently pointless, the simple mystery defiant of analysis – cricket, for example, about which nothing is ever explained and everything is always accepted. The English worship things whose appeal mystifies those who are not English: cups of tea, rain throughout Wimbledon, pubs. Similarly, the English gentleman worships things whose appeal mystifies those who are not English gentlemen: MCC ties, burning the boat that was Head of the River, nursery food. And the English country gentleman worships things whose appeal mystifies those who are not English country gentlemen: old clothes the colour of trees, concealing while revealing how rich and grand you are, blood sports.

Why, you of the classes beneath him wonder, and the English country gentleman wants you to wonder, would anyone actually want to arrive at Newmarket coursing club before 9 o'clock on a January morning, to wait for a dirty, frozen stubble of frost to thaw so that greyhounds can run without fear of breaking their legs, warming the body in a kennel of a Range Rover and the lips at a hip-flask, barking rough flirtations at red-cheeked women across the aural miasma created by dogs that howl and scream for the satisfaction of their helpless atavism? What is the *point*? There is neither setting nor ceremonial in open field coursing; there is no guarantee that anything will happen; there is no sense of occasion; there is no sense that anyone cares which dog wins. It is cold; it is uncomfortable, and it is possible that some or all of the players will end up injured or dead. But the pointlessness is, to the English country gentleman, the whole point. A simple mystery, defiant of analysis – that is what coursing is to him and that is why he loves it. It is sport, it is what it is, the reason for doing it is traced in elusive golden dust upon ears of corn in a square of field somewhere in England, the words grow again every time the field is ploughed, they can only be read if looked at from a certain angle and if you can't see them then you shouldn't be standing there anyway.

Watching blood sports always seems to me like an act of wilfulness on the part of the spectator. It seems impelled by a wilful desire to prove that one can laugh in the face of life's cruelty; a desire to prove one's toughness; a desire to make oneself less vulnerable by denying one's vulnerability, by refusing identification with victims and by engaging with, even enjoying, the harshness of life, by wearing its rough realities over one's soft flesh like a battered leather skin coat. In fact, because it takes one out of one's watchful self, and because its object is to produce victors and victims, all sport can make one cruel, callous and careless with one's feelings. I've heard men at the dogs shouting: 'Knock that fucking six dog down, knock it out you bastard' – although real dog men wouldn't say it, they don't have that desperate attitude towards winning – and the men who do say it both mean and don't mean what they say. And because greyhound racing is frivolous and regulated, what they say remains in the harmless sphere of words and wishes. In coursing, however, the sphere of the game cannot contain the vicious, deathly tangents of reality. The unpredictability overflows the predictability. That is why it is a blood sport.

I had always believed that blood sports, in their acceptance of cruelty, are no different from any other act of violence; they simply disguise themselves rather more cleverly. They replace a truly civilised quality, that of emotional identification with other creatures, with a pseudo-civilised quality, that of social identification with creatures identical to oneself. In so doing they attempt to throw a veil of good breeding, a Hermes scarf, over the fact that the qualities which are really being celebrated are anti-civilised. But I was there, that morning at the Newmarket coursing club, and for a while, yes, I wore the Hermes scarf. I went along with it. I heard my voice start to bark: a human being assuming the instincts of animals. I felt my mind begin to countrify itself, to perceive pleasure in ruggedness, in the code of behaviour which derides the new, the urban, the synthetic, and which glorifies the ability to make sport from the most natural of materials: a field, a dog's desire to chase a hare. Standing like a good Englishwoman upon that frozen earth, amid vistas of unchanging land, I realised quite clearly the febrile, grasping vulgarity of greyhound racing. Being surrounded by coursing greyhounds helped me to do so. Since 1926 the breeding of coursing and racing dogs has gradually separated, and these were clearly marked out for a more primitive purpose. Some of them must have weighed 100lb. Like boxers who move up a weight class, they looked subtly, but powerfully and dangerously, bigger than track dogs. Their thick mad necks were almost bullish, and their eyes were shielded and unreachable, like those of the people around them. Many of the dogs were a dark fawn colour, but with black muzzles, and this sooty covering, like gypsy stubble or the mask of an alien fighter, made them seem like greyhounds in a nightmare, inexplicably larger, their natures suddenly unfamiliar, their whinings not plangent but vicious, their coarsened faces dark and demonic around their snapping maws: they were frightening because they were the known made unknown.

Getting used to these greyhounds, accustoming

myself to the fact that these were not my babies who played at killing but fighters to whom love meant nothing, helped me to put the battered leather skin coat over my soft flesh. I prepared to engage with, even to enjoy, the harshness of life. I prepared to accept, even to laugh at, to drink a 10 am toast to, the fact that reality can be cruel. I prepared to deny vulnerability. It was only a hare, for Christ's sake, I began to want to think. And, as the charming coursing people had explained to me, proferring a seat in their Range Rover, a swig at their hipflask and a chink-of-light entrée into their social sphere, they did not want the hare to be killed. 'She' – yes, the hare is always 'she', we don't really know why, do we? – 'she' is very rarely killed, 'she' almost always gets away. And it's so much more exciting than track racing! That's just a *gambling* sport. This is the real thing, just wait and see.

So I did, but I couldn't bear it, not once the coursing, the thing that everyone was there for, had started. This is how it works. Two slavering, yowling greyhounds are held at the neck until the hare has been beaten out of the bushes, and has run about eighty yeards ahead. I remember several English country gentlemen baying in rhythm, *ordering* that their desire be fulfilled and that their voices terrorise the hare into thinking that its safest course is straight ahead. The dogs are slipped from their noose-like collars. They hurl themselves towards the hare which, realising that although speed will not be enough, nimbleness may be, turns in an attempt to disorientate the dogs. The first dog to force the hare to turn is given points, and points are awarded for subsequent turns, so coursing is won not just by speed but by agility. A judge, following the action from atop a horse, disentangles the visual miasma, the stopping and swivelling and scuffling, the desperate desire and the desperate fear. A powerful stillness hovers above the spectacle, far higher than the judge, untouched by the urgent men, the screaming dogs, the wild feet upon the earth; it is as if time is suspended while it waits to see whether the hare will live or die.

It is very hard to convey what a hare looks like on its straight run down the course. It looks very real, very furry, very alive – never more so – and the panic of its flight is very exciting to watch. Somehow it also looks frozen. This may be because its eye is so fixed, a glinting bead of immobility. Each bound of its legs propels it further than seems possible, and so fiercely that it seems the hare must trip over its own extremity of motion. The sound of its feet upon the earth is like the beating of its heart. Its turns are untidy, tatty, unrhythmic. Sometimes it makes so many of them that it dances itself perfectly between the two dogs, who can then pull it apart like a Christmas cracker. After an hour of the coursing, contrary to what I had been assured, I had seen two hares die. Small streaks of dark red were painted as if by a sick child, with pitiful feebleness, across the welter of mud, ice and grass, where their ignoble memory was gradually churned into the earth.

It is the pointlessness that I find least bearable about any of this. The idea that coursing is closer to the origin of necessity in sport than racing is, in fact, a hollow persuasion, as much of a sham as the hipflasks and Hermes scarves; coursing is pointless, and that is its point. The

English country gentleman is above points. The things that he does have no point beyond simply the doing of them: an attitude towards life which entails living in an eternal present and believing that past and future will always be identical. What could be more different from the dog man, with his leakily sentimental heart wrapped up in his shrewd and cynical body? How could he begin to comprehend this wilful incomprehensibility, when his sport is so aggressively, so magnificently obvious in its appeal, so dependent upon the hope that the future will be utterly, wondrously superior to the past? Never again, after that morning in Newmarket, would I think of the true dog man as anything other than a kindly, candid creature. Lary, vulgar, flash, let him be all those things if he wants to be. His unmysterious yearnings are pure and clean and honest compared with those of the English country gentleman.

It was an English country gentleman called Lord Orford who established the first official coursing club, at Swaffham in Norfolk, in 1776. Many more such clubs followed after, for the sport was hugely popular, patronised by monarchs as well as aristocrats (a couple of centuries earlier, Elizabeth I had had the Duke of Norfolk draw up a code of conduct for coursing which largely subsists today). In 1836 the first Waterloo Cup, which was named after the hotel in which the draw for the event first took place, was staged at Altcar in Liverpool, across the fields of the Earl of Sefton. This cup soon grew from an eight-dog to a sixty-four-dog event and is still the most important coursing event in Britain. But, as it grew, so naturally it changed. It did not preserve itself pure and intact as an ideal. From its beginnings as an event, it quickly became an Event, and as soon as an event becomes an Event then it begins to have a point, and usually that point is money.

The popularity of the Waterloo Cup made greyhounds rather like horses, something to spend new money on. Those middle-class migrations into the secret worlds of the aristocracy which took place, in great mannerly shoves, throughout the Victorian era are evinced even in the annals of the National Coursing Club studbook: I can almost *see* the very silver hipflasks being produced from the handsome tweeds that flanked the countryman's arena, can see the unignorably rich figure of Leonard Pilkington (of glass, chemicals and Widnes) happily discussing his newly amassed troop of twenty-six coursing dogs with the Earl of Sefton and Lord Lurgan*. These greyhounds were an asset, they were a way in, they were an interest, they had a point; as always when a phenomenon becomes the least bit publicised or celebrated, people were rushing towards it in the hope of finding something they could get out of it.

Thus with coursing. First came the nouveau riche; then, inevitably, came their roguish relations, the lary old boys that they had wanted so much to leave behind. Here they were, muscling in, looking for a bit of action, looking to make a bob or two. This was the end of the nineteenth century, by which time a growth in the working man's income had led to a concomitant growth in gambling: upon the Earl of Sefton's unchanging land the bookmakers erected their stools and boards, and before them stood their mesmerised followers, money outstretched, eager to pay whatever it took in order to win. For even the smallest surplus of money imbues people with the urge to play capitalistic tricks with it. The sensible ones invest it wisely and the excitable ones gamble it foolishly. The sensible ones connect the surplus with the rest of their lives and the excitable ones play with it in the breathless, ravenous, disorientated, unseeing way that a child plays with just-opened toys on Christmas morning. As with all addictions, the rest of life stops when the gambling starts.

A shout from the crowd, growing every moment more excited as the short drama is about to begin, proclaims the fact that the hare is in the battleground and is about to meet his Waterloo. And higher still, and louder than all, the raucous cry of the bookmaker, 'Take 7/2', 'Take 2/1', rises shrill in the air.

This is part of a letter, sent in 1911 to a journal called *The Humanitarian*, from a member of the National Anti-Gambling League: was it the atavism of the crowd or the opportunism of the bookmakers that caused him the most offence? Or did he feel that the hunger for money blunted the sensibilities to so worn a level that killing seemed less important than winning, that the sharp agony of the hare disappeared beneath the confused, clamorous desires of dogs and man? If that was what the writer felt, then he may well have been right, for passion is an enemy to morality. But better the passion that kills for the sake of something than that which kills for its own sake. Of course, the coursing establishment was appalled by the irruption of the bookmaker into its ancient sport: the coursing Stud Book recorded in the

1880s that 'the objectional feature of betting' as prac-
tised by 'bookmakers, thieves, welshers and blackguards'
had 'developed itself to such an extent as to be a
thorough nuisance'. What that means, really, is that the
death of a hare was perfectly acceptable as long as it was
perfectly pointless.

Yet one understands the mixture of panic and disdain
that must have gripped the Earl of Sefton when Scouser
O'Toole, the Liverpool Layer, started squatting on his
land. One understands the feelings of helplessness
which swell the throat of any sporting amateur when he
perceives the forces of professionalism to be surround-
ing him. For as soon as even the *thought* of money takes
possession of something, it can never be exorcised. It
can only be contained. The real and materialistic world
had penetrated the mysterious fortress of the English
country gentleman, and by 1892 the National Coursing
Club could be seen to be trying to contain the effects of
money upon its sport. Its written constitution addressed
the problems of judges who take a 'financial interest' in
the outcome of the course: ancestors of the corrupt
phantoms that would haunt greyhound racing from its
first to the present day. And how can they not, when
money is involved?

One understands the attitude of the coursing establishment, although it still feels odd to me that it should
object to gambling and not to killing; one understands,
and more easily, the attitude of the letter-writer to *The
Humanitarian*. But his implication, that there is a connection between the demoralising thrills of gambling
and the demoralising thrills of blood sports, is in fact
only partly true. Most coursing men – who, having had

more than enough all their lives, had never known what it felt like to overflow with a sudden surplus of money – despised gambling. And although some gambling men loved, and still love, coursing, to many of those who betted with the bookmakers it was an irrelevance whether the hare lived or died. Or no, not exactly an irrelevance, in that they preferred that it should live; they were tough men, not cruel ones; but given the choice what they would *really* prefer would be something a bit more ship-shape, a bit more up their street: a race rather than a course, perhaps, like that Hendon job a few years back, with the dogs chasing something a bit less unpredictable and pitiable; something they could run after properly, something controllable, rather than that poor bloody hare with all its bobbing and weaving. For these gambling boys were, of course, the origins of the dog men. They went to the coursing because there was a race within it upon which they could have a flutter, but they were amiably baffled by the country gentlemen who went for the sake of the sport alone. What was the point of that?

The worlds of coursing and of racing, the ethos of each sport, could scarcely be more different. Yet in the fifty years between the first two British greyhound races, the one at Hendon and the one at Belle Vue, the dogs was nurtured within coursing. When greyhound racing started, in 1926, all the dogs that ran in it were coursing dogs – usually the rejects; all of them were owned by coursing owners and all of them were trained by coursing trainers. Until the dog men took over (which began to happen almost immediately but did not take full effect for a few years), coursing gave of itself to the dog men's sport. There is a photograph, taken at Belle Vue on greyhound racing's opening night, of four greyhounds, held by their subdued, servile-looking trainers, whose owners are recorded as the Duchess of Sutherland, Lady Cholmondley, Lady Maidstone and Lord Stanley. Five years later they would be almost completely supplanted by businessmen, bookmakers, dog people, but it is extraordinary to think that it was these aristocratic patrons who made possible the birth of one of the great working-class sports.

Of course, there was no reason for them to believe, at that time, that dog racing was ever going to be anything other than an occasional, amusing diversion from the yardstick of coursing. They may not have known that they were uniting with a tradition of whippeting which had been growing amongst the working classes for the last seventy years or so; that, before Belle Vue opened, whippets were where the *real* fun was to be had. Cheap little poor men's dogs, frail little flyweights, patchwork scraps of ribs and eyes and courage, whippets were kept as the working pets of working men, dogs to be raced in town wastelands. Whippets were no coursing greyhounds, set at a distance from the working man by the fact that they were owned by the people that owned *him*. Whippets belonged to the men. They were dog men's dogs. The success of the dogs was absolutely the success of the men. And to be able to *own* one's sport in that way is, as I have said, one of the strongest ties that bind: bringing, as it does, the love that much closer.

The tiny, tough whippets were a source of pride such as flapping greyhounds are for their owner-trainers today. Some men would let them lie about the parlour and sleep in the children's bed; some, the tougher, more businesslike whippet men, kept them kennelled in the backyard. The first were the men who above all else loved their dog to win; the second, those who would rather fiddle with their dog for money than run it honestly for prestige. These two types still exist today; as do the corrupt phantoms which had already cast their shadows across coursing, and which were now dancing like demons within whippet racing, skulking and scheming, looking for that glorious opportunity to get ahead of everybody else. It was in fact so easy to pull a stroke as to be ridiculous. In the late nineteenth century whippet meetings could be quite well-organised, but without proper checks and weigh-ins, it was impossible to stop people tampering with dogs. All you had to do was give a dog a meal before a race and it would be out of the running. Or you might tie up its toes, or even its balls, if you were one of the naughtier, nastier boys, more in love with the bookmakers than with the dogs.

Could this be called sport, when a man didn't know whether he was backing a trier* or a sausage-stuffed creature with taped-up testicles; when a man might win more races with a scrubby old whippet that nobody wanted to tamper with than with some crack dog worth several weeks' wages; when men who couldn't lie straight in bed were in complete and unassailable charge? It is almost as if there were two different sports taking place. There was the sport of dog racing and there was the sport of trying to find out what was going on behind the dog racing – in those early whippeting days was born the need for dog men to be *in the know*. To be in the know! To have that tasty little extra bit of inside information that would place you in the very centre of the magic circle, that would put you right there with the biggest of the big boys. The 1894 dog man who knew that a whippet hot shot was actually a whippet full of hotpot, the 1994 dog man who knows that a pup who did an incredible trial in Ireland is running tonight in an A8 and that he'll be at least 5/1 – these men are two of the same breed.

And this was the sport, the sport of miners and dockers and hangmen*, the sport of waste grounds and common land and Hackney Marshes, which was to marry the sport of the Lords Sefton and Lurgan and Derby, the sport of estates and farm fields and unimaginable acreage? It is incongruous – perfectly English. One can almost imagine a Punch cartoon, 'The wedding of Her Grace, the Duchess of Sutherland and Scouser O'Toole, the Liverpool Layer', one side of the church full of faded tweeds, disdainful lorgnettes and elegant, muscular greyhounds; the other teeming with loud checks, bowler hats and sharp-eyed, scrawny whippets.

But the final push, the one that would deliver the dogs from the belly in which it had been gestating for the past fifty years, had still to come. Greyhound racing could not be born until the oval track had been invented. This was the last, essential development, which would transform the dogs from coursing by proxy into racing by right, from a blur of unassimilable speed into a real contest: into sport. The bends on a greyhound track are the rogue factor which can throw any race into disarray. They are surely what caused Winston Churchill to call the sport 'animated roulette'. They demand that a greyhound be more than just fast. They demand that it be capable of negotiating the track, for it is one of six dogs that are hitting bends almost simultaneously and at almost forty miles an hour, and it has to find gaps, avoid trouble, accelerate, decelerate, use its head, use its strength, above all be lucky. What the shape of the greyhound track really means is that every dog in the race has, in practice, a chance of winning; and there can be no higher recommendation for a gambling sport.

However perfectly English the dogs may seem to be, whatever the place that it keeps in our popular social history, the fact is that the first modern greyhound race was not the familiar one run at Belle Vue, Manchester in 1926, but an unknown, unimaginable one raced round a track in Tulsa, Oklahoma, in 1921. Neither is Belle Vue the oldest greyhound stadium in the world; that is St Petersburg in Florida, which was built in 1925. For me it was an American who caused the dogs to be born, a sports promoter named O. P. Smith, who had the idea of racing greyhounds round an oval track. He had staged coursing in Utah, had taken out a patent on the mechanical hare first used in Hendon in 1876, and had, after several attempts, finally launched the dogs upon the eager ex-servicemen of America, with whom the sport was an instant and huge success.

The oval track was brought to Britain by a friend of O. P. Smith, an American named Charles Munn (at almost the same time another American − with the wonderful name of Swindell − was attempting to launch the sport in New South Wales, helped by a dog man priest. The first track to open in Australia was Harold Park in Sydney, in 1927). In Britain, Munn formed the GRA with a coursing man named Brigadier-General Alfred Critchley, a property man named Sir William Gentle and a starting capital of around £25,000. The final push had come at last. Legitimised by the establishment, endorsed by the money men, greyhound racing started off with the right people behind it. It was to become a sport for the working man, but the more leisured man was willing it to succeed.

The GRA did in fact lose £50 on the first night at Belle Vue. But that was the last time for a long, long while – perhaps for fifty years – that it would lose money on the dogs. *It* at least was gambling on a winner. And *The Sporting Chronicle*, the foremost sports newspaper of the time, knew that it was. 'SUCCESSFUL NEW VENTURE' it sang out above its full front-page coverage. 'Greyhound racing, the pursuit of a synthetic hare mechanically propelled around an oval track, was introduced to the sport-loving people of Great Britain with marked promise of prosperity ... There were capital performances by the dogs ... People who had not visited the place during the public trials* were obviously much impressed by the elaborate setting and ceremonial, and also by the importance attached to the sport throughout. It certainly is a dignified game ...'

What an extraordinary account, when one compares it with the sixty-six years of accumulated, familiar, complex repetitiveness that goes into the front page of today's *Greyhound Life*. It is like reading a report which says '11 men on each team fought hard but honestly for the ball ... the cold but cheery crowd applauded long and loud when Accrington Stanley's plucky Number Ten player kicked the ball into the net in fine style ...', as compared with today's daily to-and-fro, pro-and-con minutiae of Arsenal or Liverpool, long ball or passing game, flat back four or sweeper, love or money. Reading that front page of *The Sporting Chronicle* makes one feel that nothing can ever feel quite that new anymore. The media of the late twentieth century, which purports to reflect life but which now has infiltrated life to such an extent that it is often only reflecting itself, simply does not allow newness to breathe so freely or so independently. It smothers it and smudges it with irony and familiarity, with comforting sneers, with earlier deposits in its own Media Bank, which take the power away from the creators and put it into the hands of the observers, making them cynical before they have ever been innocent. There is, say what you will, an innocence about that first night of greyhound racing at Belle Vue. Despite the worldliness, the gambling, the anticipation of scams and strokes on a sizeable scale, despite all this there was hope in the hearts of the dog men, who had at last got a sport of their own to love.

4

Mick the Miller and After

And it was Mick the Miller who justified the love: magnificently and eternally. Even now his body stands, stiff and stuffed and as fascinating a thing as I have ever seen, in the Natural History Museum; what a phenomenon he must have been, marching on the dog men with his unprecedented confidence and abilities, casually giving himself to them as an unsought legend, that his corpse should have been thought worthy of display among all those selected representatives of the species. I actually couldn't believe that he would still be there when I went to try and find him. I hoped, though, I hoped – and there, suddenly, he was, at the end of an aisle in a glass case, looking with his glass eyes down the length of a corridor as if it were a track that he might still run down; and people were still drawn to stare at him, and people still knew who he was. With the intense but panicky delight of one who discovers that a secret love is, in fact, appreciated by others, I listened to an American telling his tiny son that 'this is a very, very famous dog'. Mick! I thought. I thought that only dog men knew about you now, but here is this young man propagating your legend to a child who may, one day, remember standing in a museum before the only animal exhibit who had a name of his very own.

Mick the Miller cuts an ambivalent figure in his glass case, a symbol of the short-memoried modern world set amid all that timelessness. In one sense he is the representative of the most highly-developed breed of dog, he is the representative of the physical capability of the dog, he is all dogs. But in another sense he looks as if *he*, not 'the dog', was the physically capable one. Unbeautiful, almost unremarkable, somehow fully sentient, still carrying the achievements of his life with him, he looks, finally, representative of nothing so much as himself.

And this was what the dog men loved about him. Like all the greatest sporting heroes, Mick had that strange quality of separateness which made him look as though he, and he alone, could do the things that he did; yet at the same time, when he did these things, he took the dog men with him. He looked irrelative, yet he invited identification, because he ran in the way that the dog men felt that *they* would run were they in his place. They too, they felt, would be able to negotiate a track, to use their heads, to find gaps and avoid trouble and go inside and outside other dogs as they chose. They too would have that supernal quality of acceleration which could lurch them into another dimension. They too would give the whole of their heart* every single time they raced. They too would run scenarios, fictions, dramas.

And they loved Mick too because he was *not* beautiful, because he did not look like a classic winner, a world record breaker, a sporting myth who would make his followers lose all consciousness of themselves in their desire to see him win. Most of all they loved him because he looked like one of them: rather plain, rather ordinary, low and rangy about the head, compact and finite about the body, invulnerable and streetwise about the eye – Mick the Miller was, as I have said, a working-class hero.

He had come over from Ireland to contest the 1929 Derby and had, in one of his heats, become the first dog to break thirty seconds for the 525 yard course. Twenty years later, dogs would be breaking twenty-nine seconds easily, but at the time Mick was seen almost to have ruined the Derby with his ridiculous superiority of pace. 'It is useless looking anywhere else for a winner', drawled the *Greyhound Evening Mirror* fatalistically; and it was right, although at first it seemed that it was not to be. For the 1929 Derby was run twice. In order to ensure a clear race, only the first two from each semi had qualified to run in it, but even so, at the first bend, three of the four dogs managed to collide and skid right across the track, leaving the fourth – who was not Mick the Miller – to trundle home quite unchallenged and very much in his own time. Mick was not yet adored in the way that he soon would be – he was the young pretender, not the good old boy, he was Red Rum when he beat Crisp in 1973*, not when he swelled a collective heart to breaking point in 1977 – and so one cannot accuse White City stadium of bowing to the will of the crowd when it declared the race void and demanded a rerun.

Reruns were used in the early days of the dogs to protect the punter and the owner from the fact that these greyhounds were coursing animals who had not been bred to negotiate tracks. Only the rarest of them, the Mick the Millers, were able to track with ease and intelligence, an ability which still could not wholly protect them from bumping by other, more bullish dogs. Before the breeding of greyhounds changed them from coursers to trackers – which didn't happen until the 1950s – dogs were far more liable to fight and cause general mayhem than they would now. Still it is hard to say whether the reruns were a good or a ridiculous idea, because it is, in fact, impossible to know whether the races that were being declared void would be considered today completely acceptable or complete jokes. One suspects the latter, otherwise the tracks would have been rerunning every race about ten times in an attempt to give every dog a clear run – at least until they realised that the element of bump and scuffle is an essential part of the frustration that keeps the dog man in love with his sport.

Anyway, Mick the Miller won the rerun Derby, and then won the race again the next year. 50,000 people saw him do so. They were captivated now by this almost human-looking dog and his unfussy displays of greatness, although they could not know that he was doing something so remarkable that night in 1930 that it would be emulated only once in the next sixty years*. The *Greyhound Evening Mirror* described how 'the manner in which Mick drew away from his opponents at the first [bend], and the amazingly clever way in which he hugged the rails and took the bends, evoked yells of admiration, and as the favourite passed the winning line three lengths in front of his nearest rival Bradshaw Fold, the ecstasy of the crowd developed into a terrific crescendo of cheers. One of the most delighted spectators was the King of Spain, who vociferously applauded the wonderful performance.' Two days later Mick the

Miller nipped across town to West Ham, where he won the Cesarewitch and set a new world record for 600 yards. He then went immediately to win the Welsh Derby in Cardiff, where he set a new world record for 525 yards (in the recording of these times he was, of course, merely breaking records that belonged to him anyway). In six weeks he had set four world records, a feat which has never been equalled, and in six months he had run thirty-four races, finishing second in four of them and winning twenty-nine of them, nineteen of which wins were in consecutive sequence, a feat which would not be emulated for another forty-four years.

Today, a greyhound of this superior ability would be nurtured; it would have its career planned, with peaks and plateaux, as if it were a human athlete. But even up until the 1960s, dogs were being run in any race that they were good enough to win – and running out of any trap. Nowadays, as has been explained, greyhounds are assigned to the traps which suit their style of running – a much safer system, in that if a dog wants to slither along the rail or skitter out to the edge of the track then it is much easier for it to do so. Nevertheless, the conditions in which greyhounds raced in the early years of their sport proved their toughness, their ingenuity and their indisputable talent.

In 1931 Mick the Miller won a third Derby but, in an irony whose bitter aptness I should prefer not to have to savour, he lost it on a rerun. Running what was, in effect, his fifth Derby final, at the age of nearly five, exhaustion finally overcame him and he finished last. I suppose one should almost admire White City for its obdurate adherence to the rules, in the face of the boos and howls of 70,000 children who did not want the fairytale to be over yet; but I should hate to have been the steward who judged one of the dogs in the race to have fought, the man who lit the red button and extinguished the creation of a truly untouchable myth. Not every dog had been knocked out of the race. Only one, Seldom Led, had been impeded by the fighting dog, and it was indeed Seldom Led who went on to win the rerun Derby*. Even so, it is hard to say that Mick – so very clever, so very determined, so very, very fond of victory – would not still have won the race on absolute merit, even had Seldom Led had his clear run. This is what I like to believe, anyway.

These stories, these fictions, these heart-swelling dramas always threaten to end with a cruel disappointment; but we know that such scenes are always penultimate. We know that the true finale will always be a glorious triumph. It is only right that Mick the Miller's last race should not have been the 1931 rerun Derby final, that it was instead the 1931 St Leger final which, at over five years of age, running in a distance further than he had ever before attempted, he won with all his old cunning and will. Nothing, nothing, nothing would convince me that there was a soul in that stadium which was not praying for that last victory. Just to think about the dog crossing the line in front makes one's heart crack with sentiment: it is easy to imagine the waves of love that enveloped him at that moment, to hear the cheers of purest pleasure as he stood for the last time upon the winner's rostrum. Mick the Miller had been the emperor of a cynical, worldly populace, had reigned over a sport fuelled by selfish desires, but he had made his subjects want to subsume themselves into a collective, innocent purpose, that of 'going to see Mick', of 'hoping Mick would win'. He had united the dog men, and he had given to their sport a strange, sweet dignity. Still they would hold close to themselves their private, individual love affair with the dogs, but Mick the Miller had proved that they were all, nonetheless, loving the same thing.

More manifestly, he had given the sport an identity, a name, a face. He had given to greyhound racing its own rough and ready kind of fame. By the 1930s (a decade in which attendances rose from 17 million to 26 million) it was bristling with an earthy glamour which rubbed against the earthy anonymity that the sport had always tended. Mick had brought the night and the world to the dogs.

When he appeared in a 1934 film with Flanagan and Allen called *The Wild Boy*, he severed greyhound racing's final, imagistic links with its ancestral worlds of coursing and whippeting. The dogs had always been the lover of the dog men; now it was starting to act the part, to dress up for him, to sparkle and dimple and signal its fascination. It had become a film star, a celebrity, and it was attracting film stars and celebrities to itself: Amy Johnson, Gracie Fields, the King of Spain, Prince Bernhardt of the Netherlands, all of them coming to scent and disseminate the smell of real human pleasure. It had engaged the attention of the world. A foreign journalist described the crowd at White City on Derby night in 1936: 'There were belted Earls, young men fresh from public school, officers and all ranks of the fighting forces in mufti, clubmen, sportsmen of every rank and file, businessmen, clerks, railwaymen, labourers and indeed (keep it quiet) a sprinkling of clergy.' Now the world would come to the dogs and the dogs would become the world. Now it would be more than just sport, more than just an ordinary part of life that was also an escape from ordinary life. Now it would always be yearning towards the lights, towards the city, towards not just money but the visible signs of money, towards celebrity, towards glamour. The dog men themselves might still slope into the stadia in flat caps and trilbies, puffing on a soggy Woodbine, faces pinched and quenched by life, but their heads would be full of ineffable desires. They would be great urban dreamers. They would stand beneath and before those lights which poured themselves so generously into the stadia, and which gave to the tracks the look of stages, of film sets, upon which the dog men were almost, but not quite, performing. Beyond those lights, somewhere behind this real yet theatrical world before them, what unimaginable other world was there, if they could only penetrate it?

This is the effect that greyhound tracks can have upon the spectator. A stadium like Walthamstow, with its intense effusions of light and life, can seem like a magical palais of urban dreams. How to explain, to those who have never felt it, the joy of those nights of cramp and bustle, of shouldering one's way through seething, shifting crowds, of shimmering with the sense of belonging, of seeing hope be born and die twelve times in a few hours, of the hunger for life and hope and money and fun and victory that these nights both satisfy and create? How to explain the way in which that stage, upon which one almost, but not quite, performs, can come to symbolise the life which one almost, but not quite, lives?

Walthamstow stadium, which was born around the time that Mick the Miller was coming to the end of his reign, was an urban dream in itself. It was the creation of a Hoxton bookmaker named William Chandler, a bold, impressive man, a *real* man, who created himself as surely as he created Walthamstow: with nothing but a brain as sharp and quick as a flick knife he had become the number one bookmaker on the track at White City, then, in 1931, a director of the new Hackney stadium, from which he sold his shares to pay £24,000 for a flapping track in Chingford. This fourteen-acre site is today the foremost track in Britain. It is still run by the Chandler family – now third generation – which is a dynasty that seems to create for its members an inescapable destiny. Grown Chandlers still talk of 'Grandfather', are still overawed by the energy and personality of the man who still seems to run Walthamstow stadium: the family has refined itself to the point that its Hoxton origins are entirely invisible, but Walthamstow still reeks of a gaudier, gutsier glamour.

On Saturday nights one can scarcely move for the bodies of young East London and Essex people, breaking as rhythmically as waves into renewed spills of rich laughter, knowing less about the dogs than about how to have a good time. Saturday night at Walthamstow is almost purely a social occasion, and the dog men are less in evidence. The racing is not so important as the people who have gone to watch it, which makes the atmosphere slightly imbalanced, slightly uncontrolled. But the gaudy, gutsy glory of Walthamstow can still entrance; on big nights especially, when the glamour of the racing is equal to the glamour of the stadium. Then the place seems to shudder with life. I have never been anywhere that feels as intensely alive as Walthamstow can sometimes feel; nor anywhere that makes *me* feel more alive, hemmed in as I am by fervent men whose eyes are dancing with the lights of the stadia.

A perfect Walthamstow night, very recently: my father and I at the final of the classic Grand Prix. Limitless champagne – the Grand Prix is sponsored by Laurent Perrier – within the chrome and mirrored conservatory of the Ascot Suite*: a long black tunnel studded and beaded with thousands of lights like a jet and diamond bracelet. A slither away from all this privilege toward the bars filled with the jaunty eyes of Essex boys and the would-be shrewd eyes of dog men, which stare hungrily at the GUEST badge on my right breast. Outside into the quickening air for the big race final, standing at the very edge of the track and – with that same feeling of dislocation that I get when I see actors close up – trying to connect those real bodies with the spectacle that they are creating. Over to Charlie Chan's, the nightclub that belongs to the stadium, whose immaculate and sheeny interior is filled with young people in clothes worn so proudly they must have been bought that very afternoon. Dancing in the middle of the floor amid loops of energetic ease, of hilarious vigour, of unrestrained noise, of unthinking happiness. Marvelling at the simplicity of life, sometimes.

Back in the 1930s, while Walthamstow dazzled to the east, White City glowed in the west. White City was GRA owned but it, too, was the creation of one man, Major Percy Brown (being full of military men itself, the GRA loved to employ them in its stadia, presumably to impart some rigour and cachet) who managed White City from the early 1930s until 1972 and who made of it the touchstone against which all other stadia would be measured. Major Brown, who died in 1992, was a forth-right but charming, opinionated but wise man who had started his career in greyhound racing as a part-time tip-ster on a Manchester newspaper. He really knew his dogs – was a tremendous racing manager – but he also understood the potential power of White City to become a totem of smartness, of courtesy, of earthy elegance, of robust restraint, of genuine glamour; and he was the perfect man to realise this power, for he had, in equal parts, an obsession with the upholding of standards and an ability to create ease. And he was, like William Chandler, helping to create something that was both en-tirely new and entirely desired. Could that ever be possible again?

Throughout the Second World War the dogs was adored with all the fervour that is given to an object that might, at any time, be removed from its lover. The sport had, of course, been banned at the outbreak of war – all those lights, pouring unstoppably over the cities! – but after a while it was allowed to continue, greatly reduced, during daylight hours – a concession which saved the lives of large numbers of greyhounds, although many had already been destroyed. It is a testimony to the power of the dogs that it managed to keep going during the War, when kennel and stadia staff were being called up, transport to and from meetings was minimal and there was a great deal of opposition to even its limited continuance. 'Is the Home Secretary aware', thundered Herbert Morrison (Tottenham, Labour) 'that women working in munition factories for twelve hours were having to walk two or three miles to their homes because conveyances were filled with people going greyhound racing?' All the puritanism and self-righteousness of which this country is capable came surging out against this harmless diversion; photographs of *full carparks* at Harringay were printed in the newspapers as if the owners of these vehicles had driven to a devil-worshippers' convention. But despite the fact that the dogs, during the War, comprised nothing more than a small number of stadia staging only one meeting a week, overall attendances were still very high. At the beginning of the War they were 26 million and by the end of it they were 50 million. There was nothing else to do, of course. Sportsmen had been called up, so there was no football, and all other fun was on hold; but that is still a great many people going to the dogs, fighting their way on to the airless buses, dodging the bombs that were falling on to the cities and hitting the tracks at Wimbledon and Romford, braving discomfort and danger in order to keep an appointment with their lover.

My father was a very young man during the War, working not fighting, and it was then that he first started to go greyhound racing. 'Everybody used to go to the dogs. There was nothing else to do. There was only work. It was the only entertainment we used to have, to go to the dogs on a Saturday afternoon.

'I got a couple of dogs with a friend of mine. We got them from Aldridge's, the auction place at King's Cross. There used to be a sales there, Irish and London dogs. And we had some kennels and we used to look after them. Well, there's nothing to it. You only have to feed 'em and keep 'em clean and walk 'em. And we made a lure, a bike with the back tyre off and we wound a rope round it and pedalled it in, a rope with a skin on the end – that was to train 'em with. We're talking about flapping now. We used to get a taxi to Henlow, but it wouldn't take us all the way, we had to walk the last couple of miles. Well, it made no difference to the dogs. Of course, people that were in the know didn't use to do that – the taxi drivers would take them. But we were only young lads. And we fed the dogs with contaminated meat – I mean, if animals died, you'd have that meat for dogs. And for some human beings as well, there was plenty of it sold.

'We used to race at Skimpot* as well. I think that was just after the War. That was quite a nice place, it was one of the better flappers. It had a stand and a buffet out the back. It didn't look much from the outside, but you had to kennel the dogs at Skimpot, there was a vet – oh, it was a properly constituted track, it was no better and no worse than they are today. The bloke that owned it, he used to rule it with a rod of iron, I mean he was quite an upmarket bloke.

'We used to go to Skimpot on Saturday afternoons to see if Old Tom would get beat. Old Tom, he was this fawn dog, and he was unbeatable. He won about fifteen races on the trot. They used to bring these dogs down from London to beat Old Tom – "He won't win this Saturday, this dog's so-and-so in London, it shouldn't be flapping" and one thing and another, and Old Tom would be 4/1 and the London dog'd be evens. He was always a fair price because there was always something he couldn't possibly beat. And bugger, he used to win

85

every time. There was one man who used to bring cracks down from London just to beat Old Tom. And the whisper'd go round, this dog is down from White City. But Old Tom just used to win. He was a good tracker, and he didn't like losing.

'It was sport, wasn't it? You went to the dogs. You got what you wanted. A track, and a stand, and you stood and you watched. Prior to the war, greyhound racing was very near the number one spectator sport – millions and millions went. . . . After the war, there were other things – telly, all manner of things came on the scene, didn't they? Though it was still big in the sixties and seventies, for that matter. But it was declining, always declining, after the war.'

What was it like when you first went, I asked my father.

'Not much different to what it is now, really.' For it is not the dogs that has changed, but the world that used to come to it and that it used to become.

During the decade before the war, the dogs had exercised the power of unconscious strength. During the decade after the war, it exercised the power of conscious strength. This was what is known as the Golden Age of greyhound racing, when owners, dogs and stadia were never more attractive. Their sport by then was fully established, a fact of life, its newness no longer remarkable; and it must have seemed quite indestructible, for it had survived the war, the fuel crisis and the 10 per cent Government tax on Tote betting. Now it was ready to celebrate with Britain a bacchanal, a knees-up, a glorious revival of the days when the dogs had reigned unconsciously, carelessly supreme.

Throughout those years of loosening after privation, rich owners and their dogs overflowed with liberality toward each other. George Flintham, a property millionaire, who had bought his first greyhound in 1929 as a railway worker bewitched by the forbidding magic of White City, owned sometimes as many as a hundred dogs at a time and reached ten Derby finals with them, although he never won the race; Noel Purvis, a shipping magnate who had spent £5 on his first greyhound in 1927, gave £2,500 for Derby winner Mile Bush Pride (the value of the dog was considered to be of such interest that the cheque with which he was bought was printed on the front of an Irish newspaper); Al Burnett, a nightclub owner, who named his dog Pigalle Wonder after his Pigalle club in Piccadilly, won the Derby with him in 1958; Frances Chandler, daughter-in-law of the man who created Walthamstow, owned a string of great greyhounds, including St Leger winner Magourna Reject and Laurels winner Polonius, all of them bought for her by her husband as birthday and Christmas presents. The dogs of these people were some of the finest ever to race, and they ran at a time when competition was at its highest. These owners were animated, glamorous people who created a kind of egalitarian oligarchy within greyhound racing; their wealth, their dogs, their fame set them apart, but they always retained a graceful submission to the power of the sport that they loved, and an instinctive identification with the other people that loved it too. They were flash, but they had no pretensions.

Compared with some of the dour dullards who own dogs today, drooping inside market-stall blousons and talking self-important nonsense to *The Greyhound Life*, these people cut a bit of a dash. Flintham was known as the Aga Khan of greyhound racing. Al Burnett asked that Pigalle Wonder be brought on to the track for the 1958 Derby final like a sultan, by four flunkeys, a request which Major Brown refused. Frances Chandler was a ravishing woman whose bold but dainty beauty and position in the greyhound racing world must have made her an object of complete adoration with all the dog men; my father always talks of her as 'quite a handsome woman', which in his reluctant idiom means staggeringly good-looking. There is a photograph of her, taken some time during the 1950s, in which she is kneeling beside Magourna Reject, a very strong, alert and combative-looking dog dressed in his St Leger winner's coat. Mrs Chandler's high heels sink neatly into the grass. She is entirely elegant in her tight skirt, her chic neck scarf, her hooped earrings, her full make-up. The huge Essex house in which she lives with her family and her racing dogs blossoms in the background. How adult, how womanly she looks, compared with the fluttering anaemics, the powerless gamines, the tracksuited androgynes, the sexless aggressors of today; how different in provenance seems her beauty; how much of that world of urban dreams it is, how generous, how real, despite its immaculate sheen. In the 1950s the immaculate sheen *was* real. Even today, in her seventies, Mrs Chandler embodies that kind of stalwart femininity. Even today she reminds one of what the dogs would have looked like in its Golden Age.

But during the Golden Age the dogs was slowly dying, although you would never have believed it unless you had seen the attendance figures. Like a man who is stabbed from behind and who walks on, unaware of his mortal wound, the dogs was outwardly quite unchanged. In fact it never seemed so alive as during the years of its conscious power, when its life blood first began to drain away from it.

My father says that during the Golden Age he would go to White City, stand on the terraces and be unable to move. But even then, although as many people as before were attending each meeting, there were fewer meetings. Then there would be fewer people at these fewer meetings. The decline of the dogs, the wound that it had sustained at the hands of the changing world, would start to show itself; the all-powerful colossus of a sport would begin to look marginalised, diminished; and never again, except on Derby nights, would it be impossible to move on the terraces of White City. Nevertheless, the years of the Golden Age had ingrained greyhound racing into the British psyche. In the days of its unconscious power, when the dogs was new and strong, the sport had created itself as it went along; but in the days of its conscious power it knew exactly what it was. It was a setting for players in the real world.

Today, when people are not so much players in the real world as players in its images, the British psyche has, naturally enough, an image of greyhound racing. This image is not exactly inaccurate, but it is somehow completely wrong, for it turns the real world with which the dogs was engaged into an *image* of a real world. 'Realities' like money and gambling become almost pantomime symbols, which only 'types' of people deal in. A film like *The Blue Lamp*, a Rank sociodrama in which a young thug (Dirk Bogarde!) who has shot a policeman is finally cornered in White City stadium, reflected the world when it was made in 1950; but today it unconsciously propagates this imagistic view of the dogs. Perhaps that is how people *want* to see the sport. In which case, how is it possible to explain to them the absolute reality of the world with which greyhound racing is engaged? It is not possible; yet that is the most important thing about the dogs. Certainly it is impossible to explain it in a book, even a book which insists upon the absolute reality of its subject matter, for even such a book must at the same time be creating images through words, distancing the actuality of the world.

For example: as soon as I say that Peter Alphon and James Hanratty, the two suspects for the A6 Murder* in 1961, were dog men; that in evidence Hanratty mentioned how he had spent August Bank Holiday morning at Hendon greyhound track; that Peter Alphon's alibi for the murder was founded upon a visit to Slough dogs; that Alphon heard the news of the guilty verdict on Hanratty when he was at White City – as soon as I say all this, *I* start thinking of greyhound racing in an imagistic way. How fascinating, I think, what a marvellous thing to put in the book. Hanratty the petty crook, Alphon who lived hand-to-mouth by gambling – how typical of the dogs. How *real*. I can just *imagine* it. But the thing is, of course, that it *was* real, that there was a time when those things really did happen, that they were part of the lives of these men, that they were simply things that they did: a thought which can sometimes be one of the hardest to assimilate.

Because, from the first, the dog men actually created their sport, it was not something that they knew as an image before they knew its reality; they *made* its reality. And because it was created a very short time ago, and it has been handed down through the dog men to the descendants who comprise so much of the dog world today, greyhound racing still retains traces of its true atmosphere; the influence of William Chandler, Major Brown and the millions of unknown dog men is still very near. But, as I say, although the dogs has not changed, the world has. The dogs and the world began to part company after the war, when young men who would previously have thrown themselves into an inescapable love affair with greyhound racing became more careful with their identities. Other activities, other sports, made the men more important, made them feel that instead of being part of the world they were part of a separate, select section of it. Television and newspapers, as they grew in popular significance, highlighted this feeling. Affiliating oneself to something that was italicised by the media could make one feel most separate, most select, most important of all; for it targeted you directly, you personally, and you as a member of a vast and connected world.

And indeed, since the Golden Age the dogs has scarcely featured at all in the popular media. During the years of unconscious power, Mick the Miller could be written about as if he were any celebrity – Amy Johnson, Gracie Fields, Alex James, Ramsay MacDonald, the King; there was no funny business about him being a *dog*; he was, quite simply, famous and deserving of fame and it was assumed that, as such, people would be interested in him. Yet at almost the same time as this jaunty comedy was being played out in the press, and

Mick the Miller was becoming one of the best-known names in the country, the BBC* was refusing to broadcast the Derby final live on radio. 'In view of the peculiar responsibilities of the BBC and the exercise of its public service monopoly, it is not desirable to include commentaries on greyhound racing.' One has to say that this puritanical stance is typical of an organisation that sometimes seems to know very little of the way in which real people live their lives; typical too of the way in which such unworldliness views the dogs, seemingly all unaware of the fact that greyhound racing is no more and no less corrupt or corrupting than any other business.

But the dogs has always had to put up with such nonsense. Here is part of a letter to the *Guardian* in 1932, protesting against the opening of Walthamstow stadium: 'Greyhound racing has no qualification to be called a real sport'. Here is the *New Statesman*, pompous as a bullfrog, holding forth in 1946 with its opinion that all those who go greyhound racing are 'going to the dogs'. Still today the 'quality' newspapers refuse to cover the second most popular spectator sport in Britain: anything but dogs and darts is the policy at *The Times*. If you were to ask these po-faced people for their reasons, they would probably start telling you that they cannot approve of gambling (although they never seem to say that about horse racing), or that they know the sport to be crooked (of course, nothing else is). But I don't believe that those are the real reasons. I think that the loftier type of media person is, quite simply, unwilling to understand the way in which ordinary, undramatic people lead their lives. It is a kind of snobbishness, and therefore a kind of deliberate ignorance. The only way in which the media people can deal with phenomena like greyhound racing is by distancing them, by turning them into images.

But the media did give its glancingly intrigued attention to greyhound racing during the 1980s. This was partly because of the appearance, in the middle of the decade, of two dogs whose ability was so superior that standards had to be applied to them as they would be applied to any other sportsmen. Ballyregan Bob, who won thirty-two races in succession, and Scurlogue Champ, who broke twenty track records, were perhaps the finest, fastest greyhounds that have ever – will ever – run. They were two of the greatest sporting stars of the decade, as great as Coe and Ovett and, just as if they were Olympic athletes, they were kept apart from each other for over a year. They finally ran together in a bookmaker-sponsored match race at Wembley called 'The John Power Showdown', and when this race was broadcast live on *News at Ten*, it seemed almost as though greyhound racing was back in the business of producing sporting heroes. But its connections with the world are too weak for it to be able to do so any more; something about the television coverage of the event reminded one of the quirky little story in *The Times*, more than a hundred years earlier, about the two greyhounds that were chasing a fake hare in Hendon. (And even had the media been genuinely ready to herald greyhound racing as a great lost sport, the Showdown was such a Letdown – Scurlogue Champ retired injured after two bends – that the dogs probably blew its last chance with the telly boys that night in 1985).

No, it was not really Ballyregan Bob and Scurlogue Champ that interested the media in greyhound racing, although these dogs may have helped to draw its attention to the sport. What the 1980s media *really* liked about greyhound racing was that it was the perfect subject for those distancing, ironising, pseudo-analytical pieces of style commentary with which the decade pullulated and which spilled their bad seeds over into the years beyond, with ghastly and cynical effect upon both the media and the world. Most newspapers seem, throughout the 1980s, to have had a journalist on their staff who was smitten by the idea of writing about the dogs, and most editors seem to have thought this an unimprovable idea. There the dogs crouched in its corner of the British psyche, in its backroom of British social history, familiar yet unknown, comprising elements of worldliness and dodginess and obsessiveness and lariness and parochialism; it seemed just impregnable enough to be worth cutting open, and just pathetic enough to fall apart at the incisions from what was now the real world. How confounded these commentators must have been when they encountered the flat, shadowless, enclosed entirety of the dogs. How wrong they had been – although they were never going to admit it – to think that this would be easy to write about.

But if the dogs itself was hard to transcribe, its image was not. The commentators could take the unmysterious yet complex world of greyhound racing and fray it out into a circle of familiar notions; target its heart with their blunt arrows that hit everything and touch nothing. And they had their effect upon a fashion-obsessed era which would seize upon anything around which it could weave a cult. During the late 1980s, City boys who had been gambling all day with currency futures would go east to

Walthamstow to gamble all night with dog futures. Ex-public school boys from Parson's Green would take tables at Wimbledon, mock the sillier greyhound names and stare with openly appalled amusement at the dog men. Cellular phone companies would hire the Ascot Suite for clueless evenings of corporate hospitality. Lary men trying to waste unkoshered money would straddle the stadia bars like Henry VIII, cold eyes within a jovial face, cold jewellery stuck upon hands like implements, buying greyhounds as if they were used cars, selling them as if they were scrap metal. Young couples desperate for something different, some new conversational material, would go to the dogs for an unusual night out. Young men would hit Walthamstow and Charlie Chan's on a Saturday night like hand grenades to show what impeccable Essex boys they were. I get very protective of the dogs when I see these people coming at it from their other lives, blithely ignorant of the painstaking accumulation of detail that has created both greyhound racing and the lives of the men that follow it. Ridiculous, really, because a decent dog man could wipe the floor with any bumptious interloper. But still there is the unconscious vulnerability of his childlike heart, his urban dreams, which no interloper should tread upon.

Of course the stadia, strangled and squeezed by falling attendances, courted the popular media and its followers with the assiduity of an actor wooing a casting director. Bugger the dog men. In with the pine and taupe, up with the chrome and mirrors, on with the pop music. String the bars around with televisions, put them on every table, repeat each race, once, twice, in slow-motion, so they don't have to watch it while it's happening. That is what the world has made them used to. That is the future of the dogs.

Or is the future of the dogs even closer to the television screen, even further from the world? Is the future in fact a betting shop as serenely well-equipped as a hotel lounge, as comfortable as a home, in which one can always see exactly what one wants on the television, no argy-bargy over the remote control: just seamless greyhound racing on SIS, all day, all night? At the beginning of 1993, the Government announced that it would be legislating to allow the evening opening of betting shops throughout the summer months of April to August. Greyhound racing had feared and fought this for some years, although it had always believed that it would eventually happen. If racegoers really do – and it is, let's face it, the modern way – give up on the effort of going to the dogs, of connecting with the world beyond; if they really are willing to pay 10 per cent betting tax in exchange for the convenience of being able to nip round the corner and watch telly in William Hill's nice quiet house; then greyhound racing is in a desperate position. It seems impossible that some tracks should not close*.

Meanwhile, the betting shop bookmakers, particularly the Big Three – Corals, Ladbrokes, William Hill – are in a fine position. They have been fighting for evening opening almost as hard as greyhound racing has been fighting against it; and they have won, because the Government's share of the off-course betting tax is 7.75 per cent, and the more bets that people strike in the betting shops, the more revenue the Government will receive. But the bookmakers were already in a very strong position, even before the decision was taken on evening opening. Before tax, they receive (as of the early 1990s) an estimated £1,600 million in off-course bets on the dogs. Of this, about £3 million* is returned to the sport. Horse racing is threatened by lack of money, yet it gets a far better deal than the dogs: of the £4,000 million that is gambled on the horses, £48 million returns to the sport. This is because horse racing benefits from a levy that was negotiated in 1961, when betting shops were first legalised, as a means whereby the bookmakers would compensate the sport for any subsequent loss of revenue. Believing that betting shops would never be used by more than a marginal section of the population, greyhound racing did not bother to negotiate a levy in 1961; and it has certainly never had the chance to do so since.

The organisation of greyhound racing has been characterised, throughout its history, by a lack of foresight, by an inexplicable faith in the sport's ability to generate income. Recently things have changed. Since the mid-1980s, when it seemed quite possible that greyhound racing would not live out its human lifespan*, it has tried to run itself like a modern business, to 'market' itself, to make money; but it has left this change of attitude perilously late. It has renewed the fight for a levy, whilst fully aware that it is its own fault that it did not negotiate one when it had the chance. It is its own fault, also, that it ever allowed the Big Three bookmakers to buy tracks, especially BAGS tracks, at which the bookmakers now stage races so tight and impregnable (sometimes with eight instead of six dogs) that they are quite blatantly being run for the benefit of their betting shops. It is, again, its own fault that in 1976 it stopped the NGRC from centrally negotiating the BAGS contracts with the bookmakers. Tracks which had thought they could get more money for themselves than the NGRC had previously obtained simply lost their contracts; the bookmakers then bought stadia of their own and awarded BAGS contracts to those. And it is partly its own fault that it had, by the 1970s, allowed itself to become so financially pulverised that it had no options left but to sell, sell, sell – sell what was best about itself, sell those tracks that had leapt to embrace the dogs in those breathless days of the late 1920s, sell what symbolised its days of unconscious power. Greyhound racing, the love of the dog man, had not noticed that the dog men were dying off, that they were being replaced by the money men and that the money men love only one thing.

It is not, however, the fault of greyhound racing that an indifferent government is permitting eager bookmakers to open their betting shops at night; that those long, sweet, summer evenings, Derby night evenings, will no longer belong to the dogs. Does this mean that the future really will be one in which Leisuretown betting shops are full of men watching television, and Leisuretown stadia are full of men and women watching television? Will the links really be severed, after so comparatively short a history, between the dog men who stood, unwanted and embarrassed, beside the bookmakers on the Earl of Sefton's land; between the dog men who walked their tiny, tough whippets through the grimy northern streets; between the dog men who felt quiet stirrings of fascination as Mistley won the first ever greyhound race in 1926; between the dog men whose hearts broke with sentiment as the five-year-old Mick the Miller won the St Leger in 1931; between the dog men who took their greyhounds flapping during the indomitable daylight wartime meetings; between the dog men who roared home Pigalle Wonder and Mile Bush Pride to the great Derby victories of the Golden Age; between the dog men who felt the intense effusions of light and life at White City and Walthamstow and dreamed their urban dreams; between the dog men who stuck to their sport, who took their children to their sport, when the world began to change and leave the dogs behind; between the dog men who can be seen, tonight, sparsely circling the stadia like black specks on a join-the-dots drawing – a tenacious breed of men, keeping their heads down, all the better to study the form? While there are still dog men, inhabiting the present, creating their sport by their indifference to doing so, the links with the past *cannot* be severed. While there are still dog men, there will still be the dogs; and while there are still dog men at the dogs, the dogs will not change; however much the world changes, that used to come to it and that it used to become.

The High Life

I first entered the world of White City in the 1970s, at the age of nine or ten. Every person who went there seemed to me then, and seems to me now, to have been truly grown-up in a way to which I still aspire. In the days when my father owned up to forty greyhounds at a time, my life was punctuated by visits to White City, just as, I suppose, those of my friends were punctuated by visits to pony clubs and tennis clubs; I think myself very lucky to have been breathing the air of such a large and liberal world instead. This world lives now inside my head, and my mind blinks almost every day with the flashes and pangs of sudden memory when I see a smaller, duller life around me: people with the faces of incurious voyeurs; people listening to the robot's roar of a Walkman; people choosing the video that they will watch that night; people watching MTV in pubs; people drooping and shuffling round leisure centres; people dawdling round minimarts, or service stations, or any one of those vast shops which squat like suburbs at the side of the North Circular Road; people pretending to have fun; pretending to have fun myself – sitting in a wine bar waiting for the love stories of girlfriends to end or for the man I am with to buy me a drink – thin, gutless evenings that will never yield memories. Or I might be reminded of that other world by an image of my parents' fine and easy position within it: a photograph of my mother, standing on the White City track in evening clothes, smiling as Zsa-Zsa Gabor presents her with a trophy, behind her the dark night and the melting lights, before her the exhausted triumph of her brindled boy, the whole gleaming with a kind of stalwart glamour. I am a child again when I dream this world back into life, a child staring at the grown-ups and waiting for the day to come when I shall be one of them.

Of course White City was not really a place for children. At the time I always felt a bit of a damn nuisance, trailing my gawping bewilderment around all that worldly bonhomie, longing to go down to the trackside and look at the parading dogs instead of sitting like a facsimile adult in the restaurant, slumping bored and exhausted after the last race while around me spines were determined and erect – but wouldn't I love to be going to the place now. How well I feel able to approach, to savour, to live up to its earthy elegance. I'd go there three times a week with pleasure; there is nowhere that I would rather go. But of course White City no longer exists, and even if it did I suspect that its straitened white spaciousness would have been made over in the image of a leisure centre, that its robust, careless steak meals would have been replaced by unwieldy structures of lasagne, that its sophisticated, ribald, resolutely social, dog-talking clientele would have been ousted by sets of stiff and silent courting couples looking for a new night out, sticking pins in the racecards and betting in neatly-piled pound coins.

The name of the place tells you all you need to know about it. It is a perfect name. The vast white shell was indeed a city, harbouring within itself great numbers and diversity of people in what was somehow an egalitarian hierarchy: stratified though it was into the upper, middle and lower classes, the restaurant, the bars and the terraces, still everyone was united by the dogs, the sport, the place. They were all good citizens, for they loved their city. They respected it. They formed its identity even as they submerged themselves in it; it was a city in which atmosphere was created by the willingness of the citizens to submit themselves to the atmosphere. But the city was not a haven from the world; it *was* the world. When one went to White City, one was the world, and one was communing with the world. How else could the citizens have that unconscious air of being grown-up people leading their grown-up lives? – so different from the way in which people sometimes look to me nowadays, adults with the social ineptitude of children, the shambling gait of adolescents and the disengagement from the world of zombies; cynical, as I say, before they have been innocent.

The restaurant at White City opens inside my mind rather distant, a warm pink receding interior, chilled with silver and crystal and with gently jangling gin and tonics. It reminds me of Harrods beauty salon as it used to look when I was a child, before it was recast in chrome and cane and it lost all its mystery, its magical, dreamlike quality of a grotto that would open into unimaginable spaces – or maybe I just ceased to be a child. In the White City restaurant sat the dressed-up grown-ups in their evening clothes and their winking jewellery, their air of restrained yet infinite prosperity made all the sharper by the laughing constancy of their moans about Harold Wilson and 'the taxman'. The rich dog men mingled with an odd mixture of celebrities – Diana Rigg, Frankie Howerd, Roald Dahl, Roger Moore, Ted Dexter, Robert Maxwell – all of them enjoying the same air, the same gracious government by their city. Of course as individuals they weren't so sparkly and mysterious as all that, not at all, some of them were quite plain and deadly, but in their willingness to submit themselves to the sparkle and mystery of White City they emitted a collective glamour, a glamour of an old style which was dying, really, before the 1970s and which may have finally died with them. It was a very English glamour, redolent of London telephone numbers preceded by exchanges called Flaxman, Gerrard and Park, of dressing-up to go out as a natural, necessary business (when my mother presented a prize one night at White City, she did it in a long dress and long earrings; when I presented one at Catford in 1990, I did it in black jeans), of pushing one's personality outwards in continual bursts of regulated energy, of conversations that were woven out of the stuff of the world rather than that of television, of quiet largesse, of tasteful swank, of controlled impropriety, of kindhearted toughness, of compassionate capitalism, of the days when greyhound racing was a colossus of a sport.

At the centre of the restaurant was an enclosed, two-tier, glass-fronted, suspended compartment containing about ten tables. This was known as The Box, and to be sitting inside it was to be perched at the very top of the social structure that White City – and thus greyhound racing – then encompassed. The Box was reserved for big owners and celebrities, those that were especially favoured by Major Brown and his successors. As a child, I didn't quite realise that this was such a desirable place to be and that several adults would envy me my seat, although I inferred something from the jewellery that my mother chose to wear and from the fact that, on Box nights, my father would drive to White City in the Rolls Royce that he normally affected to dislike. All I ever wanted to do was to get down to the trackside (in my ballerina dresses and hair slides, standing among the bookmakers with my feet in fifth position) and wish our greyhounds silent luck. But this, of course, was not Box behaviour. If one was inside the Box one thought oneself damn lucky and damn well stayed in it.

The atmosphere within this sealed compartment was cool, crisp and rarefied. From without, it looked almost like a definition of separateness and privilege, inset as it was into the midst of the teeming city like a still centre, a painting: configurative, lucent, entirely visible, entirely impregnable.

If the still centre of White City was The Box, then its animated centre was what I called The Room. The Room was quite a small sitting room behind an unimportant door somewhere in the private middle of the stadium, where endless flights of drab stone steps would open suddenly and mysteriously on to the public throng. It was the place where friends of the city governors went drinking after the city gates were officially closed. Again, what wouldn't I give to be in there now – except that I wouldn't be. 'We only got in there when we were big time', said my mother. In those days, at the end of each race meeting, I prayed that we would not be going in there. But I would see the conspirator's smile on the face of the General Manager, and I would hear my father's voice, trying to sound helpless, disarmed, as if the decision he had just taken had been ordained by fate, saying, 'We'd better have one more for the road', and the door to The Room and to a serried cluster of bottles, dimpling and twinking in the dull light, would be open again. I would sit there, aching with boredom, and watch the grown-ups at their incomprehensible play.

I can't remember any of the people in there. I can only remember the feel of the thing, which was social in the extreme and which celebrated the qualities of urbanity, worldliness, fun and the ability to drink a great deal without becoming vulnerable. On emerging from The Room, my mother (who had to drive) and I would watch the change of air hit people like an uppercut as they made their serpentine descent of the back steps to the carpark. Now I would be one of the drunks. Then I thought the whole thing wildly tangential to the business of the dogs. I wanted it to be tomorrow morning so that we could be at the Hook Kennels and back at the heart of things.

The only thing that I liked about The Room were the photographs on its walls. There was one of White City, taken when it had just been built for the 1908 Olympics. It looked very similar to how it looked nearly seventy years later, but in the picture it was dignified by emptiness. That suited it. Its elegant white façade was stretched like a thin sheet over its simple structure. It looked like a sporting venue, there was nothing else it could have been, but it looked, too, like a benign and rigorous protector, housing and gazing down upon the men that overran it. Another photograph was of a man called Dorando Pietri, an Italian who had competed in the 1908 Olympic marathon. He had been first to get back into the stadium, but he had collapsed just before reaching the line and had been helped to stagger over it by spectators. For this he was disqualified. The picture shows a tiny creature in shorts that flapped like huge handkerchiefs, with arms that hung like Petrushka's, supported at the crook of each elbow by men in coats, hats and moustaches, surrounded by a concerned and galvanised crowd, the winning line a few, impossible feet away.

The last race to be run on Derby final night at White City was always a two-circuit open called The Dorando Marathon. Yet the incongruous ease, the unflinching speed, with which the greyhounds ran their thousand-yard race made this a somehow strange – albeit stylish and sympathetic – tribute to the man. There is a dimension to human sport which that of racing animals can never enter. In the photograph, Dorando's face expressed the agony of one who stands at the edge of the gap between absolute desire to do something and absolute inability to do it. Empathy with this complete and terrible consciousness of one's limitations, one's mortality, one's impossible longings, is a private and vulnerable emotion, silently shared by human beings; it has nothing to do with the admiring, worshipping, frustrated love which a man might give to a horse or a greyhound. Whatever other emotions one may feel for the racing animal, there is no empathy possible with that self-contained, purposeful, beautiful, fundamental lack of self-consciousness.

*

Although this lost and adult world breathed its own life into White City, White City created the atmosphere within which it was able to breathe. Like the Hook Kennels, it was tightly, sharply organised. Maybe it was because it had always had army men in charge of it, but its carpark attendants conducted themselves like tank commanders, its commissionaires were as bossy as field marshals and its restaurant was run like a military campaign. The maître d', Mr Bertelli, was a long femur of a man who managed to make of deference a kind of terrorism; anyone who thinks that dog racing is all about lary old boys whose clothes have fallen off the back of a lorry should have met Mr Bertelli. He was the best, most elegant, most naturally imposing maître d' I have ever encountered. Nowadays, of course, one is meant to resent that kind of orderliness – indeed, at the time, my father was given to weekly confrontations with the doormen when they refused to give him his owner's pass ('That old sod', he would say afterwards, 'he knows me as well as he knows himself'). But the truth is that it worked. As with the Hook Kennels, it gave the place a dignity within which one felt that the right to relax had been earned. And White City was never snobbish. It wasn't like Ascot, cringing before lordliness and herding the proletariat into pens. It ruled *everybody* with a rod of iron: it governed all its citizens in a respectful way that made them want to be respectful back. The only real division was between those who knew about the dogs and those who were completely ignorant; but even this fundamental difference was smoothed away by White City, which was not just about being at the dogs, but about being in the world.

Occasionally there were intruders upon that taut and earthy serenity. My father: 'I can remember some aristo being there and showing off like billy-oh. And I went and saw Mr Bertelli about him. "What can I do, Mr Thompson?" he said. "They'll never come here again."'

That particular evening, when the aristocrat in question went to White City with a bunch of his cronies and attempted to draw the attention of the entire restaurant to himself, while pretending to disdain and ignore all around him, I recall very clearly, although I wasn't there. My parents came home laughing and shuddering with disgust and for some reason we have never forgotten why; I think because the party had been trying to impose its alien world on to a world that we understood. But what did they actually *do*, I wanted to know now. 'Oh, nothing really, but they were just so dreadful. They were throwing breadrolls all over everybody, he was shouting and screaming. They thought they could do whatever they liked. It was quite unbelievable.' As indeed it must have been, not in itself, but that such a nursery-minded incursion should have been made into the adult urbanity of White City.

Ted Dexter also got thrown out of the place one night when he tried to run round the track, but that was only an aberration. Dexter was, in fact, something of a dog man, who subsequently went in for training greyhounds of his own, and he was not sent into permanent exile. I always rather admired him for actually doing the thing that must surely cross the mind of any lively dog person. And bad behaviour of that kind, which was against the laws of White City but was perpetrated by someone who nevertheless knew and respected those laws, was rare enough to be forgiven. It was like the night when a friend of my father's, Jerry H, a huge drinker who used to make a fire of his bill when it was presented to him at the end of an evening, had a greyhound disqualified for fighting.

My father: 'That's when he went and called Percy Brown a drunken whatsit – he'd got some room to say that. He bought this dog. It was a silver brindle, I shall always remember. Nice-looking dog. We were in Ireland, and this bloke, its owner, had it in a final that night – well, Jerry wasn't going to let it run in a final, in case it showed too much form, he was going to buy it. We had somebody with us and he said leave it, but Jerry was determined to have it. He only paid £200 for it. That did about 28.70 round White City – that could run. But the man tipped us the wink. Because it was a fast greyhound, but to buy that for £200, you knew there was something wrong with it.

'It fought like a tiger and it got disqualified – that's when all the trouble started. Jerry walked straight up to Major Brown. Major Brown didn't take any nonsense, he had plenty of mouth. "*Did my dog fight?*" said Jerry. "Course it bloody fought," he said. "Fought like a tiger" – which it did, everybody saw that. It nearly ate the bloody dog. "You drunken bugger," Jerry said. "Look at it, running out of your eyeballs." And then all hell broke loose. How he didn't get barred I'll never know.' I should say that he didn't get barred because, for all his transgressions, White City knew that he still knew what it meant to be one of its good citizens.

Certainly it didn't have to bother with pandering to

those that would never understand what it meant to be good citizens. The sycophancy that an aristocrat would inspire in other worlds was quite inimical to White City, with its stately yet careless self-assurance. After all, it had had the Duke of Edinburgh there a few years earlier, when a dog running in his name won the 1968 Derby, although the story is that he *was* pandered to by the stadium. The Duke was a perfect citizen, even a putative dog man, and sycophancy towards him was quite unnecessary, although surely tempting. But this was the only occasion I can think of on which White City's steely principles of high-toned egalitarianism were betrayed. The Duke's greyhound, Camira Flash, had finished fourth in his Derby semifinal, but the third-placed dog was disqualified, having been judged to have fought. This errant behaviour was regarded as a god-send by a management that would normally have censured it with vigour. It meant that the Duke could have his place in the Derby final. Camira Flash took over the slot vacated by the fighting dog and, at a price of 100/8, running from the dreaded trap four, won the race quite comfortably.

All the old boys down on the terraces were in an uproar, booing, shouting and hollering – all except those who had backed the dog; a lot of them had probably done their money on Shady Parachute, the 4/6 favourite, but what they were angry about was the pre-ferential treatment that had been given to the Duke. The rules of greyhound racing state that if a dog is disqualified then the one behind it does *not* move up into its place. I know all about this rule, having once backed a dog which ran second to a fighter. When the disqual-ification was announced I went haring up to the Tote, wild for my winnings, only to be told that no, my dog was not deemed to have *won* the race and that no, I could not have any money. If that had happened to me before 1968 I, too, might have been pretty cross about Camira Flash, sliding into the Derby final and then having the audacity to win it – although the thought of booing a greyhound, as it makes its proud, delicate and bewildered circuit of the track, fills me with rage. But there is no doubt that the rules were bent for the Duke, and that it was the preference given to the already privileged that had caused the booing. Nor did White City have the sense to allow Camira Flash to have set a precedent. When, in 1975, Lively Band* was disqualified for fighting in his Derby semifinal, the fourth dog, Shamrock Point, was not promoted into his place. This was particularly unfair because it was entirely Lively Band's fault that Shamrock Point failed to qualify – in rugby parlance, he took him out – and anyway, what difference would it have made to have let the dog run? If I had been Shamrock Point's owner, I should have taken a certain bitter satisfaction from the fact that my dog then went on to win the Consolation Derby* in a time far faster than the final itself.

Derby night at White City was hot with atmosphere. I feel sorry for Wimbledon, which took over the running of the race in 1985, because no one who ever went to the Derby at White City thinks that anywhere else can *really* stage it. 'Ah,' we say, 'the atmosphere, the elegance, what a terrible day when they closed the place down – bastards – nothing's ever been the same since, has it?' White City connected the Derby with the past in a way that Wimbledon can never do. The racecard was engraved with signifiers of tradition: the trophies named by Major Brown after barely remembered champion dogs of the 1930s, the Fret Not Stakes, the Long Hop Chase, or after the little Olympic runner, the Dorando Marathon. When the dogs paraded around the track before the race, their bodies, iridescent beneath the light, were streaked and shot and shimmering with the ghosts of other greyhounds: Mick the Miller, Pigalle Wonder, dogs who in some unimaginable time had been not myths but had paraded this track, had run this Derby, had inhabited this here-and-now.

White City rose to the occasion of the Derby in the way that those rare greyhounds do. Sporting occasions sometimes feel like a quest for atmosphere: one formulates excitement, watches Mexican waves through a haze of indifference, finally abnegates oneself from all that showing off and self-expression. But some events one falls into headfirst, helplessly and drunkenly. One knows that they are the real thing. One knows that all present are unified by a tacit comprehension of the significance of the occasion. They do not have to tell themselves that the Derby is an event, they do not have to try to make themselves more important than the Derby in order to make it an event; they *know* that the Derby is what matters, and this knowledge, this willingness to subsume themselves into the event, makes the event significant. These mysteries, these myths, these great traditions, great occasions: one cannot partake of their power by enveloping them in bear hugs, by French kissing them, by dancing around on top of them and hoping that other people are watching this close congress. The only way in

which to partake of them is to submit oneself to them, to
be humble with them.

And so, entering White City on Derby night, one
knew that one was both partaking of, and contributing
to, an event. One was an actor upon a stage, playing a
part, swelling a procession, watching one's own performance, watching the piece of theatre that it was
helping to create. To attend was to feel the ties that
bind: all the dog world was here, celebrating the night
on which the greatest greyhounds ran in the greatest
race at the greatest stadium; all bowed down before all
that greatness. All *wanted* to bow down before it. Their
eyes glinted proudly with subservience to the occasion.

Derby night in the restaurant meant black tie and, at
the end of June, with the sun flooding painfully through
the vast glass frontage, the early part of the evening was
always cruelly hot. My first Derby was in 1976; on that
night the last part of the evening was hot as well, though
in a different, less evil, more exhausting way. The
drought and the heatwave had a fearsome hold on the
White City restaurant.

But I had wanted to go to that 1976 Derby so much.
Since 1960 the race had been shown on television, for as
far back as I can remember on *Sportsnight*, when lights
like creamy suns melted and burned behind a beaming
Harry Carpenter – *he* knew it was an event – but for
some reason I didn't see the 1975 final. Perhaps it was
ousted from the television by a friendly football match –
England versus the Faroe Islands or some such, but at
about 7.00 the next morning I was in my parents' bed-
room demanding a result. 'If I give you five guesses, you
won't get it', said my father, which was ridiculous,

because it was a five-dog race and anyway he'd given it away with that answer. Clearly, the dog that could not win had won. 'Tartan Khan!' I said, bouncing around gleefully, asking for details of starting prices (25/1), did my parents back the dog (no), how had he won the race (easily), what had happened to all the other dogs that were supposedly so much better than he (they weren't). The romance, the *wit*, of this win by Tartan Khan strengthened my desire for complicity in this occasion.

The 1975 final had been thought to belong to Myrtown, the odds-on favourite who had run second in 1974; but these races are not run to a preordained scenario, they are shockingly, staggeringly of the here-and-now. And this here-and-now had been shocking and staggering. Only one other dog has ever won the Derby at such long odds*. If Tartan Khan had been the invention of a storyteller, one would have dismissed him as a foolish fantasy: he had been third in practically every round of the competition, and at the beginning of 1975, White City had asked his trainer to take the dog away from them when he lost eight races in a row. He scarcely won more than twice in his whole racing career. However, the two races that he won were the final of the Derby and the final of the St Leger.

After the first of these wins, every dog man in the country quested for an explanation for the sudden explosion of greatness from this mysterious greyhound. Eventually one was found. Tartan Khan's trainer had, prior to the final, walked him regularly by the railway line at Cheddington (where the Great Train Robbery took place), believing that the noise of the trains would prepare him for the noise of the crowd. Certainly on

Derby night the dog had nerves as loose and easy as Ronald Biggs's.

The noise of the crowd, what is called in the dog world the 'Derby roar', does terrorise some greyhounds. It is for them like hitting a wall of sound, built by gamblers. As the dogs parade the track, the wall is being laid in place, brick by brick, welded together by the hunger of the crowd for the occasion that is now almost upon them, oh so near, they can feel it coming, they are being encircled ever more tightly by the waves of its energy, in a few minutes, in a minute, in a few seconds they will hear the words – 'and now the hare's running' – and the encircling waves of energy will constrict them in a vice from which the only release is to shout and shout. When the hare passes by the traps the individual voices of the crowd become one. When the traps open the dogs hit the wall of sound. Some of them balk at it in fear. Some of them crash through it like heroes. Tartan Khan was such a hero.

And the next year I got to the Derby, and sat in one of my ballerina dresses, in heat that beat as intensely as in a summer garden at midday, encircled by waves of energy, my heart jumping a tiny chasm every time I looked at my watch and saw that 10.45 pm this evening was becoming first a possibility, then an inevitability. How well I remember that evening – not clearly, but powerfully. What I remember are the pink tables, the bread rolls like big shells, the curls of butter set in ice, the angled sashay of waiters with one arm aloft; the buzz of dogtalk made unnaturally electric by the vibrating timbre of each individual voice; the quality of the early evening light outside, promising such a night, such a summer; the quality of the air inside, soggy with heat, watery with electric light, bright, heavy, filmy, trailing cigarette smoke; the slow building of the wall of sound; the slow encroachment of the floodlights upon the sun; Mutt's Silver, the 6/1 winner of the Derby final, dropping to the ground like a boneless puppy and rolling luxuriously upon his pristine victor's coat; the occasion playing upon the terraces, the bars, the restaurant and The Box as if it were a strong and gentle hand, strumming the strings of a guitar and leaving them separate, tensile, reverberating and harmonious.

When it was there, it seemed as if it would be there forever. I regret intensely the fact that I scarcely bothered to go to White City after my last Derby there in 1980; but I know that if I had never gone there at all then it would be almost impossible to write this book, ignorant as I would be of this place whose high definition, whose easy grandeur, whose self-possession and self-assurance were at the heart of greyhound racing: the proud, and now buried, heart. Nor should I have in my possession the two vital code words which can unite the most disparate band of dog people. Say that you went to White City, that you saw the Derby there, that you owned greyhounds there – and that's it, you are in. At the sound of the two code words, hardened dog men relent and relax. Understanding, of a shared past, of shared priorities, flashes dimly but indestructibly. One day I may meet a dog man who does not respond to the code: 'I always hated the bloody place', he will say, 'give me Walthamstow any day'. But he will be as rare a creature as a Derby winner. White City has become an icon, a temple, a touchstone. To the dog men its obliteration caused a pain as inexpressibly deep as the razing of Lord's would cause to a cricket lover; except that Lord's would be mourned and eulogised by a world beyond cricket, and White City never has been. White City *was* the world, but those who never went there never knew it.

The Low Life

And now for a different kind of fun. In the 1970s, when I wasn't at White City, I was at Harringay stadium in North London, and even as a child I could perceive a difference in the atmosphere of the two places – mainly because at Harringay I could do what I liked. There were no restrictions on descending trackside, no ballerina dresses, no keeping silence in the midst of adult conversations. Spines were looser at Harringay, children were children and not dressed-up grown-ups. White City was elegant and respected by everyone who went there; Harringay was relaxed and easeful, with adumbrations of lariness. It did not attempt to compete with the aristocratic edifice to its right or with the aggressive palais to its left. Although, in terms of racing, and attendance figures, it was almost as important as both White City and Walthamstow, its attitude towards its own image was more casual; which made it no less atmospheric, because the atmosphere at the dogs was, in those days, created wholly and involuntarily by the people who went there.

I tend to think of *afternoons* at Harringay because it was, in the 1970s, a BAGS track with a daytime meeting on Saturdays. These BAGS meetings achieved a certain fame when they featured on ITV's *World of Sport*, a programme presented by Dickie Davies (he of the face like a twinkling, moustachioed cushion and the hair like Diaghilev's) which had been conceived as a rival to *Grandstand* but which tended to founder as the BBC showed rugby internationals, Grand Prix previews, the Olympic Games, and ITV was left with skateboarding, cyclo-cross and live competitive trampolining. But it did have horse racing, and this it made the most of by its invention of the ITV Seven, an accumulator bet in which one backed, either to win or each-way, a horse in every race shown on *World of Sport*. It was an impossible bet to get up, although apparently about one person a week did manage it; but it was a challenge, and it got people watching.

In the winters, however, *World of Sport* found that even the ITV Seven was being taken away from it. When bad weather reduced the complement of horse racing to the occasional stalwart meeting at Wincanton or Bangor, the ITV Seven became the ITV One, or even the ITV None; until the idea was conceived that the bet might have its seven limbs restored by the televising of greyhound racing from Harringay. And so, throughout the winters of the 1970s, the dogs periodically found itself being transmitted by the medium whose appetite devours all but which, for some reason, has never swallowed greyhound racing whole.

Of course television has had little nips at the dogs. The sport was first broadcast when it was, in fact, more popular and powerful than television: in 1953, when Frances Chandler's Magourna Reject was filmed winning the St Leger at Wembley. Then, in 1958, the BBC inaugurated the Television Trophy, which is still transmitted on *Sportsnight*, although it looks to me completely out of place there, like something coming from another world of which the viewers know nothing. Maybe that is why the BBC stopped broadcasting the Derby in the 1980s: only a very few people would have known what was going on or why this thing was being shown to them. The Derby is now shown on Sky television, which portrays the occasion as a whoop-up for the wide boys; but, having initially paid £1,500 for the rights, Sky, as of 1992, *receives* £10,000 from the GRA for doing it the kindness of presenting the race. Greyhound racing seems desperate for television coverage, even to the extent of welcoming ITV's 1991 comedy series *Gone to the Dogs*, which pandered shamelessly to the public image of the sport as a repository for the stroke-pulling wide boy in his back-of-a-lorry shellsuit.

The reasons why the second most popular spectator sport is transmitted only bi-annually by the most popular medium are perhaps clear enough. When a race lasts about half a minute then, unless it is being run by famous human beings, to a recognisable strategy, it is hard to be interested in it: something very quick, like a soundbite, can be far more enervating than something slow, like a story. No doubt that is why the Television Trophy is run over 800-plus metres. It gives one a chance to see a story unfold.

But there is no story to greyhound racing as it is shown on television, and to tell one would mean that the thing would have to be done properly, with decent commentators who actually knew what they were talking about; and with regular broadcasts, otherwise how to keep the story going? And that is essential; for all sport is a saga. It is like *The Archers*: miss a few episodes and when you go back to it Nelson Gabriel is a born-again Christian and Shula is an alcoholic. Miss a few weeks of football and when you go back to it Paul Gascoigne is manager of Newcastle and Luton are top of the Premier League. Miss a few years of greyhound racing, as I did, and when you go back to it not only have you never heard of any of the dogs, you haven't heard of their grandparents. Which means that until a television producer determines to turn greyhound racing into a saga – even just a seasonal one, that would be enough – the sport is doomed to flicker on to the screen twice a year, without provenance, without roots, without point.

But every now and again, in the 1970s, television actually *needed* greyhound racing, and Harringay stadium became something of a minor celebrity. Harringay's grading standards were slightly lower than White City's, so it was where the majority of our dogs raced; indeed, at this time, there was scarcely a meeting where my father didn't have three or four runners. Occasionally one of these would make it on to 'World of Sport'. This, of course, was a great thrill, playing as it did upon my fascination with the idea that these greyhounds belonged both to me and to a world outside: yet our dogs held such importance in my life that it seemed quite natural to see them on television.

To see Harringay stadium itself was like seeing our house. That was how I felt about the place. It gave me, for those two or three years when I would go there with my father and feel myself surrounded by signs of his presence – his name in the racecard, his dogs on the track – the beautiful illusion that I was at home.

Naturally enough the restaurant at Harringay threw up a different type of person from the one at White City and because things were so relaxed, especially on Saturday afternoons, there always seemed to be a lot more free passage up and down the aisles that ran the length of the stadium and behind the tables. One person who visited himself upon us at almost every meeting was John C*, a lovely man who lived in Bow. 'He was down our table all the time. But he got into trouble over money. He used to go and sell his trousers down the market to get money to come to the dogs with, didn't he? He used to make trousers, John, with his brother. I had some off him. They weren't bad. Slacks, you know. But John never had any money. He used to spend it as fast as he got it. He'd sell a hundred pairs of trousers and – whoosh – in the sky. I don't think he'd have had two ha'pennies to rub together if it hadn't been for his brother. I mean he was a nut, wasn't he, John? Nice enough bloke, but nutty.

'That uncle of his used to come down our table – everybody thought he was a millionaire. He was in trousers in a big way. John used to tell us his floorboards upstairs were bulging with money, and he had this, and he had that. "He's got so much money!" – "His house!" – "It's hid everywhere, he doesn't know what to do with it!" Well, he went bloody bankrupt. He never used to pay any tax. He used to have thousands on dogs, and everybody thought he was the richest man in the stadium. 'Cos he was having thousands on dogs when a thousand pounds *was* a thousand pounds.

'But that bloody fool that used to hang around with John – what was his name? – he was penniless all the time. He was a no-hoper. And he was a judge, he knew everything, didn't he? Mind you, he did know a bit about it. He'd come up and he'd spiel it off, what was the best bet of the night, and how it's going to win and one thing and another. He'd say, "There's no way can this dog not lead round the first bend!" And quite often he'd be right. But then he'd go on about it. "This is the one! I've sorted this out, for tonight! This one *will* win, tonight! It *will* go round the first bend – what's going to catch it?" "Are you backing it?" "Got no money". So, I mean – he was a no-hoper.

'But John used to gamble – he never had money to gamble like he gambled. Well, he used to gamble on dogs plenty, I would have thought, for a man that made a few trousers a week. He used to come and plonk himself down – "How you doing, John how've you been?" "Oooooh – money". He was always on about money, he'd never got, he was always in trouble for, and one thing and another, and I thought, ooh, what are you up to boy? Because next thing you know he's having fifties on dogs. Where he should have been having 50p. I mean, people like that, if it was the last fifty they had in the world they'd have it on a dog. That is the trouble with them, isn't it? They gamble beyond their means. And that's gambling, isn't it? I mean, I know plenty of people who don't gamble beyond their means. It can be the same as being a drinker or an alcoholic.

'They were typical Londoners, that lot, real Londoners, Cockney people. But I don't think John was a hard enough man to be a Cockney, if you know what I mean. Most of them, they're – I mean they're well-met, you know, they're all friends, and all that nonsense – but they're hardened. But John wasn't. He was an old softie. He wasn't streetwise. But he couldn't stay away from Harringay. He was a compulsive gambler, and he was a free spender. I mean, he couldn't afford to go to that restaurant every time he went. He only had a tuppenny-ha'penny way of getting a living, and it was like spending £100 a night, what he used to spend – and he'd do that a couple of times a week.'

Another regular at Harringay 'was a different kettle of fish. Ah, now, he was a shrewd old boy. He'd got money, he'd never be without. He gambled all his life, but you wouldn't see him throwing his money around. He might have £500 on a dog, but he wouldn't look in the programme to see about having it on, he'd have something else behind it before he had his £500 on.

'He was on the edge. He was just one step in front of the law all the time. He was either doing a bit of fencing or a bit of fiddling of some sort. He'd do a favour for one of the trainers – in return for a tip, wasn't it? He'd do anything in return for a tip. He was only small-time. But he'd always got a grand or two in his pocket. He wasn't a *heinous* villain, but he was a villain.'

I also recall being fascinated by a man with no teeth. 'Well, he was a shrewd old bugger, wasn't he? He used to get information, he only used to have one bet a night. He never used to *gamble*.'

And a man with a wig. 'He was everywhere, the man with the syrup. If he wasn't at the dogs he'd be at Ascot, or at antique sales. He was a hanger-on. Where there was money about, he'd be there. I've seen him in bars with lords and ladies. And I've seen him with some *real* villains, real in-and-out-of-jailers, like Big Ginger.'

And amiable, dishevelled Billy H. 'Oh, he was a villain, he wasn't a dog man. His brother was, but then you'd never know he was his brother, 'cos he was different to Bill – he wasn't a mobster. He used to have a little entourage, didn't he? He'd always got a couple of Scotland Yard police with him.'

These men wouldn't only have been at Harringay. They would have done the rounds of the dog tracks, including White City; it is just that one wouldn't have noticed them so much at White City. There, the eye was in the mood to pick out furs, jewels worn at the neck and throat, lipsticked smiles, the careful tread of the sedentary rich, thick cigars. At Harringay, it was attuned to see leather overcoats, heavy squares of gold at the wrist and finger, grins full of nervous bombast, the shambling strut, Embassy fags. But whether these men were at Harringay, at White City, or indeed at any other track, they were, and are, inseparable from the world of the dogs.

For the dogs is a place where people play at business. When people go greyhound racing, that is what they are doing. They are scheming and planning, watching and assessing, thinking, thinking about what to do with their money in order to have more of it; and they are doing all this at night, within a palais of delight, under bright lights, amid an energetic hum, with a drink in one hand and a fag in the other: they are doing it all *for fun*. That is the world of the dogs, a world in which unreal, unnecessary business is conducted with the same intensity as the running of ICI. And they are *all* doing it – not just the low lifers, the lary boys, who gamble as they live, but the respectable people, the courting couples, even the citizens of Leisuretown. They all want to go into the stadium with a few quid and come out with a fortune. That is the feeling that puts the tang into the air at the dogs. That is why it emanates that worldly aura which is so much its charm: because it is dealing in the ways of the world, in business and in pleasure. That is why you cannot have greyhound racing without the low lifers and the lary boys, because they are simply the most extreme representatives of the world of the dogs. They are men for whom business is not a separate part of their lives – a day at the office, a rush hour bus home and an evening spent thinking about anything other than work – but a part of the whole life, inextricable from the pleasure, the nights out, the fun. The dogs is a place where they belong. They may not all be dog men, but they are all at home in a world where people play at business.

There is, however, a vital difference, between those who are ignorant and those in the know, in the way that the business of the dogs is played. It is not just that those who are ignorant are backing in pound coins while those in the know are backing in monkeys; or that those who are ignorant are gambling for fun, while for those in the know that kind of fun is serious. The real difference is that when those who are ignorant – the vast majority, the hapless mug punters – bet on a greyhound, they are gambling on what they guess the future will be. When those in the know – the inner circle, the information gatherers – bet on a greyhound, they are gambling upon how successfully they have been able to manipulate the future. The majority believes that the dog will, on previous form, perform in a certain way. The inner circle knows, or believes that it knows, that it will perform in another way, and then gambles on the likelihood that this knowledge will be proved right.

Essentially, to be 'in the know' means to know that the future of a dog has been manipulated. How is this done? Let us say that a dog is an A7 class greyhound. One way or another, the trainer holds it up, takes the edge off it, lets it get unfit, whatever – gradually the dog will slip down in grade and slip out of the betting. The trainer will bide his time, let the dog appear to be sinking into mediocrity. Then, when it is set to run in an A8 or A9, at odds of 5/1 or 6/1, he will work on it, train it up, get it back to its true form, let it loose upon a race that it is far too good for and give all those in the know a delicious killing.

And that is the principle of the simple stroke which can be pulled in any sport where there is gambling upon a live object. For as long as there has been greyhound racing, there has been the possibility of pulling this stroke; and as Del*, a dog man acquaintance of my father, says, it used to happen a great deal more often than it happens now. 'When I started going dog racing, it was very basic, and very uncontrolled. There was plenty of villainy went on then. Much worse than now. Because then there were no tests.' The test is the pre-race chromatography on urine samples that was introduced by the NGRC in 1965 in an attempt to stop the unfathomable amount of stroke-pulling that was then going on. The effect was immediate and enormous; although 'Whatever they do, they'll always think up a way of beating 'em, won't they? It's the same as horse racing, it's the same as anything – they make tax laws and there's always some clever villain knows how to get round 'em. But, I mean, that test, I wouldn't say it's foolproof, and I wouldn't say it's the greatest, but it is a deterrent. They test every greyhound before a race. But really and truly, to master the situation, they've got to be tested after the race.'

The chromatography test was, in fact, originally designed for random, post-race use, but when so many samples proved positive it was decided to change it to pre-race and to test all the dogs.

'Yes, but what I'm saying is that there can be something happen between the testing and the dog running, can't there? After the dog's been tested, you can then do something with it. I'm not saying you can stand there and do it, but there are ways ... After they've tested the dog, you then kennel it up. Well, in between going from the test to the kennel you can do some naughties, can't you? It can be done. They did something in that race not so long ago, didn't they? Well, there's three of them bloody doped, aren't there? They were doped after they were tested. You see, if there's any villains working in the stadium and all sorts, I mean – and kennel staff, they ain't overpaid and if you bribe 'em they'll do anything. I don't mean all of them, a lot of them are in it because they're dog lovers, but some of these young lads are in it to get a few quid, and they might do it. They could just give a dog a titbit when they take it to a kennel.

'They do test them occasionally after the race. They have the random tests. But the chances, when there's sixty, seventy dogs running, and they say, well, we'll test that one and that one ... Of course they test the ones they're suspicious of anyway, that run way off form, but really they should do 'em all. But there's not enough money about to do it.'

The star who brought the night and the world to the dogs:
Mick the Miller in the 1934 film *The Wild Boy*

George Raft (far left) at the Stow in the 1940s.
Charles Chandler (son of William) is in the centre

Farloe Melody runs toward the 1992 Greyhound Derby trophy

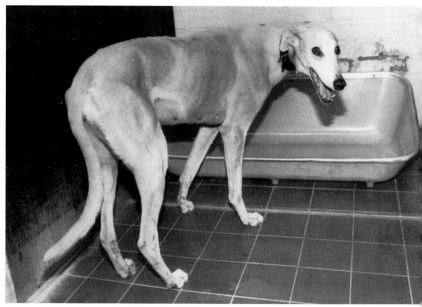
A nameless ex-racer at Battersea Dog's Home

The beloved Commutering

The vanished stalwart glamour of White City: Zsa-Zsa Gabor presents the 1972 Wood Lane Stakes trophy, won by After the Show. From far left to right: Zsa-Zsa, Frankie Howerd, Eva Gabor, Major Percy Brown, my mother and After the Show's trainer Jim Singleton

The oval arena of White City stadium

The 40 mph hurtle towards the first bend

The days when the dog men could not move upon the terraces: the final of the Northern Flat Championship at Belle Vue stadium in 1955

New Cross Stadium in 1973

And how could the men in white coats, fiddling pains-
takingly with all their little bottles in their stadium
laboratories, possibly cope with post-race as well as pre-
race testing? In 1965, when there were only eight races a
night, there were only forty-eight dogs to test, which was
feasible. Now, with twelve races plus trials, there are up
to eighty-four, which is ridiculous. So many samples, so
little time. How can one be sure that the dope testers are
reading every sample accurately?

'But dog racing, in my opinion, is as well run as anything where there's money concerned. You don't get any
sports that are clean, I'm afraid, even when they're
human beings. I mean, just look at them athletes that
have been drug taking – what a shower they are – so you
talk about bloody dog racing. Wherever there's money,
well, then you're going to get villainy. It's like any business. But then, I mean – if you go to Walthamstow and
have a pound on a race and a bit of grub and meet
people and have a few drinks, it doesn't really matter
whether the bloody dogs are doped or not, as far as
you're concerned. But it doesn't do the sport any good.'

The real value of the test – whether or not every sample is being read accurately – is that it should act as a
deterrent. Obviously the dog doper cannot be sure that
every sample is *not* being read accurately. The problem
is that, as with athletics, where drugs have become an
almost accepted factor in the sport, it is now suspected
that it is possible to administer a drug to a greyhound
that will evade detection by the dope testers. For this
reason, the NGRC is keen to spend a considerable por-
tion of its recent £3 million windfall on sophisticating
the chromatography test; which is all very well, except

that there are other ways of fiddling with greyhounds besides slipping them a mysterious pill.

Del: 'They can gallop a dog, for a start. I mean, if you've got a short runner, all you've got to do is gallop him, tire him out, and it won't do the dog any harm. Well, if you did it every bloody day it would, but four or five times a year won't hurt him.'

Or a trainer might give a dog a 'kill', let it loose on a real rabbit – that would certainly ensure its indifference that night (it would be rather like expecting a man to run half a mile at full speed towards an inflatable woman when he read the *Kama Sutra* that afternoon with his mistress). Or he might simply stop training a dog, or upset the continuity of its training, or let it get out of condition. He can't let it get fat, because it will be weighed before racing, but one knows from watching athletes how easy it is to slip from a performance peak, how easy to carry again those hundredths of seconds that one had strived so hard to shed. Greyhounds are more naturally athletic than humans, but they still have to be kept fit. It shows when they are not – they look a bit loose and listless, lack sheen and sharpness – and when they look that way they will certainly be running several spots slower than their capability. Some shrewd dog men claim to be able to tell if a greyhound is 'trying' or not from the way in which it parades around the track before a race.

So it is not difficult to fiddle with a greyhound's performance. What is much harder is getting it to find enough time to win, but not so much that it arouses the suspicions of the racing manager and the NGRC.

Del: 'But I think the NGRC tends to turn a blind eye

to the smaller tracks, provided there's no big coups and one thing and another. They wouldn't admit to it, but they know the little tracks exist by pulling little strokes. It's like the small stables in horse racing, they're the same. It's got to be proved that the racing's not straight at some of the permit tracks, but I wouldn't think there's six triers in each race. At Walthamstow I would say there's six triers in most races. It doesn't happen in the big trainers' kennels, there's too much going on there. And there's too many good dogs there. They make their money other ways. It's like businesses. Once you get a business so big that you've got people working in the office and all that, you can't do a fiddle, you can't cheat because other people are involved. You can only do that if you're a gypsy and carry your money in your arse pocket. And the same with training – you can do it if there's only you there, if you're a little compact organisation. When B. had dogs at his kennels, his head lad wasn't allowed in there before the dogs went off to the races, and B. used to go along, I'll stop that one, stop that one, sticking something in their mouths. It was a known fact. And then his head lad had to ask him, "Shall I back that one?" "No, leave that one". And sometimes he didn't used to tell him, he used to turn him over, because he wanted it all himself, didn't he, and he didn't know who the head lad was going to tell. There'd be the owner in on it as well – it isn't just the trainer, there'd be other people involved.

'But they don't just stop dogs, they start 'em. They can give 'em some sort of treatment, which is not necessarily a drug, but that gets 'em going. I mean, B. said to someone I know, "your bitch'll win tonight." And the bloke said, "Who's she running with?" He said, "I don't care who she's running with, I'll get to work on her." And so I said to the bloke, "What's he do?" He said, "Well, I don't know. I reckon he gives 'em something." But he don't give 'em anything injurious because he's got some of the best greyhounds in the country.

'I don't know what they do. Vitamins, something like that? You don't know what they get up to, trainers. They give 'em different food, perhaps? They can get up to all sorts of nonsense, can't they?'

There is, for example, a famous Irish trainer, one of the most successful in the history of the sport, whom the dog men swear can get his greyhounds to trap. It is something that they all say. What does he do to them, I asked the dog men, sprinkle them with holy water? This levity was met with a blank, or even a faintly disgusted, stare through my head. This man could get his dogs to trap, there was no argument about it, that was the end of the matter. But what does he do? I wanted to know. He's a master at his trade, they said, closing the matter again. If he's got a dog in an English final, they couldn't help but resume, he comes over here and makes sure that it gets out of the trap. Look at that greyhound he had in the Derby, they shouted. That scraped into the final, and then he came over here the week before and got to work on it, and on the night the traps went up and it was out – gone. Wasn't it? It didn't win, I said. He can get his dogs to trap, they said.

Certainly that greyhound got a flier in the Derby final, and I don't think it was because it had been walked by its trainer by a railway line. Doubtless there are ways of ensuring a fast start for a dog, just as there are for athletes.

Doubtless the Irishman is not the only trainer doing it, though because he is something of a legend, dog men like to attribute mysterious powers to him, as if he has only to lay his hands upon the dog in order to make it trap like a bullet leaving a gun. But never, ever, would you get any trainer to admit the way in which he has affected a dog's performance. He keeps secret the spells with which he manipulates the future. Only to those who are already, mysteriously in the know would a trainer admit that he has manipulated it at all.

My father: 'One of my trainers, many years ago – he was a bloody old scallywag on the quiet – well, he was in his early days. That's how he made his money, he used to pull strokes. He told me once that a man walked into his kennels and said, "I want you to win a race with this dog. I want you to win one race, and I'll give you £500." £500 was a lot of money in those days. I said, "What happened?" He said, "Well, I won the race and he gave me the £500." He made sure he won it, didn't he? He trialled the dog in and held it up until the right race came along. And then the bloke came down one Sunday morning, gave him his £500 and took the dog away.'

Trials are used for several legitimate purposes: to grade in new dogs, to bring back to race fitness dogs that have been lame or in season, and to try a dog over a new distance or the hurdles. But they are also used for one illegal purpose: to get a dog graded in at a standard below its real abilities. At each track there will be a certain grading time which a dog must run before it is allowed to race. If the dog moves track, a trainer can slow it down to the point where it will start racing one or two grades below its abilities. The racing manager might suspect; he might say, well, this dog was running A5 where it was before, what the hell's happened to it? But a trainer has several ways in which to get himself out of that one: their grading isn't as tough as ours; the track is different; the hare is different . . . Any one of the infinite variables in the sport can be cited as an excuse, and it would be very hard for a racing manager to prove that a trainer was lying.

If a dog runs a trial in a certain time, then the racing manager has little choice but to grade it accordingly. He is innocent yet complicitous – usually. In 1991 it was discovered that the racing manager of Romford stadium, Jim Simpson, was *guilty* and complicitous; that he was in league with two trainers contracted to the stadium, Paddy Coughlan and Bill Foley; that he was grading certain of their greyhounds into races comfortably below their capabilities, knowing full well that their trial times were unrepresentative; that he was having his money on whenever he knew that they were being let loose to run to their true form. He knew, none better, that, barring the accidents that can always happen in dog racing – the infinite variables – these greyhounds could not lose.*

For those few months during which the scam was being perpetrated, greyhound racing at Romford was an entirely bent business. People seem to believe that the sport is always run in such a way. But the reality is that greyhound racing is crooked in fits and starts, not concertedly. It is true that dogs are being stopped and started all the time, but only in low grade races and in a sliding scale of frequency, which descends as the importance of the track ascends – the better the track, the straighter the racing. There might be strokes pulled at the permit tracks, there might even be a gambling racing manager, but at Walthamstow there will not be; and for an organised scam to happen at a respected track like Romford was unprecedented in the history of the sport. The shock at the sheer scale of the stroke – and at the involvement of the racing manager, who must be incorruptible, or else the whole of the sport, and all one's own strokes, lose their significance – was palpable. *The Greyhound Life*, fluttering like an old lady who had just encountered a flasher, printed increasingly dramatic headlines about 'Romfordgate' every day for at least a week; at the tracks, however circumlocutory the dog talk, it inevitably found its way to the hub of things and then stayed there, tutting, lamenting, speculating, claiming to have known about it for months.

'Romfordgate' was exposed when the bookmakers had finally had enough of being stung. They got together to tap some telephones and prove what they already knew. They know it goes on, of course they know, they accept it, as often as not they are abreast of it, or even in on it, but a tickle here and there is not the same as a major coup in which all the funny money is going in the same vague direction. That had to be stopped, and had to be seen to be stopped.

Del: 'If I commit a burglary four or five times a year, the chances of being caught are virtually nil. But if I do it all the time . . . I was going to have a little coup with one of my dogs, the trainer was holding him up, but it backfired a bit, he didn't do grading time. I've been in on plenty of coups, but I don't go home and sit talking about it. Oh yes. There's one going on at the moment. It's a dog that's going in its first staying race, and we're the only people that know it can stay. We found out on the trainer's own track. Unless somebody gets on to it, it'll be 5/1 or 6/1, I should think.'

Why should anyone get on to it, I asked.

'Well, it's a job to keep things quiet, you know. People go down the kennels on Sundays and they listen. You'd be surprised the number of times dogs that should be 5/1 or 6/1 have opened up 6/4. I mean, there was a girl that used to go down the kennels, her father-in-law was a bookmaker. They do get to know.

'And people sell information 'n' all. Kennel staff, and other people that find out a little titbit. They nose about and pick up little snippets. I know a bookmaker, Rich* – he'll buy information. Jim*, who I see down the dogs, he used to go and find out for him if the dogs were trying or not. He'd earhole around, go and have a little chat and get a little bit of information, and then he'd pass it to Rich. We put him to the test, didn't we? I was there one day and Jim come up, and I said to the trainer, "Is this dog trying?" He said, "No, don't touch that tonight." And bugger, Jim was there and he was off, gone. Next thing Rich's shouting, "3/1 So-and-so", when everyone else had got it at 2s. We were on to it, weren't we? We knew.

'I'm not unfriendly with the bookmakers. It's a contest, isn't it? Which you can often win, if you've got any brains. Even though it's only bloody dog racing, you've got to have brains. Rich has got a brain. He's got a mathematical brain, because he started with his arse hanging out of his trousers, and now he backs in five, six, seven thousand quid at a time. He had seven thousand on a dog not long ago. It didn't win, no, but he managed to get himself out of trouble. He came out in front. He'll gamble on anything, take your bet on anything. It ain't just the dogs, he does the horses, the football, he's at the golf, he's at the snooker. And he's got himself into a position through his brains. His turnover must be millions. He's got a billiard room – he must have a nice house. He's got race horses. And I can remember when he was penniless. He's just a bloody old boy, isn't he? But he's bloody sharp, make no mistake about that, he's ultra shrewd. And he spends money like . . . he's ever so generous.

'That little fellow, Mick*, that's his legman, ain't it? He just goes there to earn a few quid. He does the line for Rich. He'll go up and down the line to see what money's being had on. Otherwise, when a man goes in and has £500 on a dog, by the time Rich has scrubbed the price, the punters have beat him to it. Mick's on an earn, isn't he? If Rich has a good night he'll bung him fifty, if he has a bad night he'll bung him a score. And Mick'll have his bet, and that's his night out. He ferrets out information. He'll say, "Rich, they tell me they're having a lot of money on this dog in the next race." And Rich'll put that to use. He won't take nothing. When everyone else is 5/2, he'll be 2/1, 9/4. Nobody'll bet with him. If it comes off, he'll have a skinner. He won't be paying out nobody.'

But, I wondered, don't the other bookmakers see these short odds and wonder what Rich knows that they don't?

'They've all got their own opinion, haven't they? This is the thing about greyhound racing. Churchill called it animated roulette, but it isn't really, because in roulette you haven't got an opinion. I'm not talking about your real mug punters, the ones who are more or less backing numbers – that *is* like bloody roulette. Then it's just a night out. But the dog men, they've got an opinion. If they see a racecard and see dogs run, if they know their dogs a bit, they like to be a judge of the situation. And some of them do know what they're talking about. They can probably watch six dogs at a time. Can you do that? That is the question. When I was younger I used to be able to clock 'em. I can't do it now. This is what makes a good racing manager. They can watch six dogs at a time.'

One of the finest ever racing managers was Major Brown at White City. His explanation of his ability to watch six dogs at a time, was that he wasn't gambling on any of them: 'If you back a dog,' he said, 'then you do not watch every dog in the race.' Certainly, this is true of me. If I have a bet I don't even know what has *won* the race if my dog hasn't. Del: 'Some people do, though. Jim's son, he'll say to me, "Did you see the four dog?" Well, I ain't backed the four dog, course I never saw the four dog. "That'll win next time out." And he ain't backed the four dog, but he saw the four dog. I think it's something to do with your eyes, you know. And also you've got to have a good memory, which I used to have but haven't got now.

'But when a dog man's got an opinion, then he's having a contest, isn't he? And that's what it's all about. People who go dog racing – I don't mean man and wife and kids, like they do at Walthamstow – but men that go dog racing, it's a contest. A contest with the book-makers. And if he don't back with the bookmakers, if he

backs with the Tote, it's a contest with the other people
that are there. If I'm not having a bet, I might have a few
quid on the Tote, and if I've got the inclination to sit
down and study it, I think I know more about it and I'm
shrewder than a lot of other people that go there. And so
I reckon I can nick some of their money. I'm only nicking the bloke sitting next to me's money, I'm not nicking
the bookmakers' money, but I reckon I'm shrewder than
him so I must, from time to time, have some of his
money.

'But at the smaller tracks you can't bet on the Tote,
you just can't. I always remember at Milton Keynes, I
had £20 on one of my dogs – he was about 3/1 or 4/1 out
with the books, and I don't know, I wasn't very interested in having a proper bet on him, but I had twenty
quid or something on the Tote. It paid 6/4. I never ever
backed to win on the Tote there again. If you have more
than a fiver on you're throwing money away. Of course,
it's all according whether they've got a big turnover –
you could have £20 on at Walthamstow and it wouldn't
make any difference. But if you had hundreds on it
would.

'At White City people used to have a lot of money on
the Tote, but they weren't really dog people, because
dog people bet with bookmakers, don't they? Proper
gamblers don't bet on the Tote because they'd bring the
price down, whereas at the books they bring the price
down after they've had their bet*. You get your price.
But I know when Arabs used to go to White City, you'd
get them having thousands on the Tote, they'd turn a
10/1 shot into favourite. Mind you, they never really got
into dog racing – I remember there was one wanted to

buy a dog off me, but they didn't really take to it. But if there was an Arab there at White City, one of the rich Arabs, it used to mess the Tote up terrible. I've known dogs that were completely outclassed, that'd got no bloody chance, probably be 100/8 on the Tote, and then some silly bloody Arab'd have a couple of thousand pounds on it, make it favourite. And of course, people follow that, mug punters. If they see a dog coming down in price on the Tote, they think somebody knows something.'

Surely, I asked, they think that with the bookmakers too.

'Well, they do, yes. If a dog's short with one bookmaker then that information flows around. They start saying, "Hallo, he's took a lot of money on that. Must be a live one." But then, you see, a lot of them will back a dog if one bookmaker lays it out. I'll tell you what, one night I was at the dogs. There's a girl that had a dog with my trainer, and her boyfriend was the son of Rich's penciller*. Now, the trainer had a dog running that night that in my book should have been a 6/4 shot, and in every bookmaker's book it *was* a 6/4 shot, bar Rich's. Rich was laying it 3/1. Never picked a leg up, did it. But he took a lot of money on it. They were queuing up to back it up 3/1. Nobody seemed to twig on to it, till later on – gradually they do.

'It must be fairly elementary that if you've got six bookmakers, and five of them are laying 6/4, and one of them's laying 3/1, he must have an opinion, or know something, that that dog ain't going to win. Now, there's a lot of punters that are half-shrewd. They've got opinions of dogs, but they're not as bright as all that, and if they see 3/1 on a 6/4 shot, they'll go and back it. If Rich gets a dozen bets, he's got an earn! But that dog drifted out to 3/1 with all the other bookmakers in the end. They eventually realised the dog was a non-trier. At Milton Keynes you can tell in no time at all. If you see the card, you say, "Blimey, that dog's going to be short tonight", and it ain't short, you know it ain't a trier.'

Sometimes to be seen alongside Rich, and forming with him a rather self-conscious double act, is another bookmaker, Dennis*, who went to public school. After racing, Rich will take the stage in the bar just as he did down the line, flash his thick, almost cuboid gold rings, crunch his face into grins of warm and wary amiability, and talk the compelling language of laridom. ('He's as good as gold'; 'He's a bad boy, but he'll get his uppingtons'). Meanwhile Dennis leans slightly behind him, a rather shambolic and dusty Lord Peter Wimsey, smiles at Rich with barely concealed fascination, and nurses the feelings of inner superiority that being the butt of Rich's jokes ignites in him.

Del: 'Dennis is only playing at the game. I mean, he's got a string of betting shops. I reckon he only goes to the tracks to get away from his missus. If he's got a social occasion on, then he ain't there. Then his penciller does the bookmaking. I mean, Rich hasn't got betting shops or anything. Bookmaking, taking money, is his living. But if Dennis never went to the track, it wouldn't make no difference to him, because they're a wealthy family, he's got betting shops. And he's got a lot of credit customers. He don't have to be all that shrewd. Obviously his father's a bookmaker of the old school. But Dennis is next generation, he's been educated. You don't get on in bookmaking unless you're a bit street-wise. But with betting shops ... I mean, betting shops are really a licence to print money, aren't they? Unless you get any sharpies. But if you're too sharp they don't want your money. If you win too often. Well, they don't have to take bets. There's no law says they have to take it.

'But bookmakers like Del'll take your bet. They have to take bets. The principle of bookmaking is the more money you take, the more you pocket. But some book-makers, a timorous bookmaker – there was one at Peterborough the other night, he was laying 5/2 this dog when everyone else was 3/1. And all his odds were less than anybody else's. He was just frightened to take any money, you see. There *are* bookmakers like that, they don't take threepence. They go up there, they just tiggle about, make £50 in a night and they think they've done a good night's work, whereas Rich wants to make a grand. Or lose a grand! I've known Rich to lose seven grand in a night. He'll stand there and take my bet – a big bet – and he'll shout out to all and sundry that he's taking it, because he wants people to know that he's a bold man. You've got to be bold. Unless a bookmaker takes money, he can't make money. You can't make money if you've got an empty satchel.'

Dog men feel a bond with track bookmakers. They feel that they are all playing together at the same, chancy, enlivening business: the contest, the battle of wits, which the bookmaker is destined by the laws of probability to win more often than not, but in which he is playing by the same, slightly bent, realistic rules as the dog man. The off-course bookmakers, however, are not seen to be playing by the same rules. Dog men feel that the betting shops are not content to be protected by the laws of probability. They want to win every time.

Of course, if I walk into Ladbrokes with my sweet and harmless little fiver, then that is fine; and if I walk into Ladbrokes the following day with my winning betting slip, and walk out of there with twenty quid, then that is fine as well. More often than not I will *not* be going back in there the following day. But even I, with my tiny bets struck perhaps twice a week, have been disconcerted into using two different betting shops.

I had been using the same one for only a couple of weeks when the manager suddenly said to me: 'Why do you only back Oxford dogs?' 'Because they belong to my father,' I answered. 'Oh. Only we wondered if you was getting inside information –' For Christ's sake, I wanted to say to him but didn't quite dare, if I was really in the know about these dogs, do you honestly think that I'd be backing them in fivers? The tone of the exchange was jaunty, joking, but there was a steely undertone, a sense that one had been watched, which made me realise just how carefully and cynically these betting shops are run. If they even suspect that one knows something, they will refuse the bet. If I had been backing in hundreds, not fivers, they might have refused mine. To place a sizeable bet with them is an almost military undertaking; it would have to be spread among many different betting shops, and even then one would have to be wary of the fact that they are in contact with each other. Recently a horse came in at 33/1 which had been backed fairly heavily in what was, in fact, a little coup (the owner knew that it was due to win). The betting shops simply refused to pay out. Instead they instigated an inquiry into the horse's performance. Perhaps next time I lose money in a betting shop I can instigate an inquiry into why my greyhound failed to win.

Of course there will be times when there is a clear-cut reason for refusing someone's money. But it is hard to believe that the betting shop is always capable of distinguishing between the truly dodgy bet and the one that it is simply fearful of taking. Can they really decide, every single time, whether or not a bet is being laid by someone in the know; and can they then decide that being in the know reduces the element of chance in gambling so much that it invalidates the bet?

Their control of the betting markets is such that they have, anyway, another option to simply refusing to take one's money. Del: 'If they think it's a bit live, they can blow it, take it and blow it back. All betting shops managers have got somewhere to ring up to unload. They probably go to the London office. They ring up and say, I've got a lot of money for the five dog in this race. They'll say OK, and then they'll probably have a monkey at the track. And get rid of it.

'The bookmakers offload at the track as well. If a man goes to Rich – say there's a dog at 3/1, in an open race, it's got form at other tracks, and it's a bit of a job to tell what they're going to do at another track, so he's got it at threes – if a man goes in to Rich and has £500 on this dog, his legman'll run down the line and get rid of two or three hundred quid of it. He'll go and back it with another bookmaker. And they take it, oh yeah. *They* might offload it. There's a lot of that goes on. Oh, they move the bets amongst themselves. And you might say, well, that bookmaker knows there's something wrong, why does he take it – yeah, but next week they might want to do the same thing, with Rich! They're all there to get a living. They're not – there's the odd bookmaker that no-body'll have anything to do with, but generally they all get on alright . . . I mean, they don't always take bets off each other. They might have been clobbered 'n' all, then they won't take it.

'If they've got an unbalanced book . . . a bookmaker should have a balanced book, he don't want all the money for one dog, he wants somebody to back the 10/1 shots and the favourites. And really, a proper book-maker, that makes a proper book, every time the favourite gets beat he should show a profit. The favourite should be the loser for a bookmaker. That's why, when you're at the dogs and they come in the bar afterwards – "I bet you ain't done very well tonight, Rich" – there's probably six or seven favourites won. And he'll say, "I never laid that one, I never laid that, I got rid of that" – or "I laid that bugger, I didn't fancy that at all". See, a shrewd bookmaker, like Rich, he'd have his own fancy; you know, if he thinks a dog can't win, he'll lay it. But sometimes there's one there and you think, can't see how this is going to get beat. So he wouldn't lay it – he'd lay it below the others and then people wouldn't . . . I mean if it's 6/4, he'd lay 5/4 and evens. Only mugs go and back with him then, shrewd men don't do that. They look for the odds, don't they?'

The odds at which a greyhound is quoted are an expression of an opinion of how likely it is to win, and all odds can be converted into a percentage probability. If a dog is evens (in other words, if you stake £1 you get £1 back, plus your stake) then it is reckoned to have a 50 per cent chance of winning. If it is 6/4, it is reckoned to have a 40 per cent chance of winning; at 6/4-on, or 4/6, a 60 per cent chance of winning. At 3/1, the chance is 25 per cent, at 4/1 it is 20 per cent, at 9/1 10 per cent; and when Pigalle Wonder, one of the finest dogs that ever raced, won at Wembley in 1958 at odds of 20/1-on, he was reckoned to have a 95 per cent chance of winning, which was probably about right. When the odds that a bookmaker quotes for the dogs are added together, they should total 100 per cent; but in order that, in the un-likely event of every dog being backed to win the same amount, the bookmaker should not lose out, the percen-tage probabilities always come to more than 100. That is why it is impossible that one would ever be able to back every dog in the race – something that has always attracted me as an idea – and show a profit. If they total 105, the bookmaker should be paying out £100 for every £105 that he takes – unless, of course, the favourite wins.

But a field with the prices chalked up at, say, 6/4, 9/4, 4/1, 9/2, 6/1 and 10/1 actually totals 132.33 per cent. It may not look that way, but some of the prices are too short. Del: '*The Greyhound Life* tells you the average bet-ting at the tracks, where a punter's getting the best value, and usually Walthamstow is at the top. That's the least over 100 per cent. Well, you know why that is, because there's a weight of money there. A lot of money there on a Saturday night. At some of these smaller tracks they're as much as 125 per cent, 130 per cent – they're thieving money from punters.

'At Milton Keynes, there were three open races the

other night. There was a bitch running which was a certainty on paper, and there were two others that were good things, so all three favourites won the open races. Well, they weren't value for money. I mean, that bitch, she opened 7/4, she finished 5/4. At Walthamstow she'd have finished maybe 7/4. They don't lay 'em so close. But then they're going to take more money so they can afford to be more generous. If you go and stand by them books, they're betting in hundreds and five hundreds, all the time, loads of them – where, I mean, at Milton Keynes, if a man has five hundred on, Christ, they're all falling about wondering what the hell's going to happen next.'

So: you have the problem of trying to pick, or engineer, or hear about a potential winner. You have the problem of trying to keep it secret from other people. You have the problem of trying to get a betting shop to take your money. You have the problem of trying to get the best price you possibly can at the track. The whole business of the dogs is an obstacle course in which one has to bob and weave, duck and dive, keep one's eyes peeled, one's ears pricked and one's nose to the grindstone; it is fraught, complex, almost impossible. But the gamblers want it no other way: 'it is the battle that they love, not the victory' (Pascal). They love the to and fro, the fact that, in gambling, nothing is ever finite, that things could always be just that little bit better, although they are more likely to be a great deal worse. Even those that profess not to be gamblers but calculating investors, working on a percentage, would rather be worrying about the dogs, playing at business, than putting their money in a building society and seeing it grow by a similar amount every year.

One certain thing is that, despite the evening opening of betting shops, it is the real dog men, rather than the Leisuretown inhabitants currently being lured by the stadia, that will always, as Del says, 'go to the dogs. Yes. I mean, if I've got a trier and one thing and another, if I've got something a bit special on, I don't mess about in a betting shop, I go to the track. I'm not going to lose 10 per cent, and I'm not going to take the odds after other people have got at them.

'That's the thing when you're a gambler, you must get value for money. That is why I went up to Peterborough to back that dog the other night, because I got value. I got beat, yes. But if that'd have come up, I could have had seven tickles before I lost money. That is the way to do it. *That* is the way to do it, not go backing favourites all the time – any silly bugger can back even money shots. You don't need information or nothing. I go in the betting shop Saturday lunchtime, and I look at the Hackney card and I say, well, that's the nap* today. That *will* win. That's different class. But it opens up 5/4. I don't want nothing to do with it. Because then you've got to back more winners than losers, and you can't do that.

'You can't just run dogs for prize money. Oh no, you can't do that. Not unless you've got top open racers. Well, you can do it – but you won't make no money out of them. But I've always got a bit of money that pays for the gambling and one thing and another, and sometimes I show a nice bit of profit. I mean, my trainer owes me a lot of money at the moment for bets I've had. I've got a bitch, if you backed her every time she's run you'd show a profit: she's won at 20/1 and 10/1. That's thirty bets you can have before she wins again. And her brother –

he don't like getting beat. I don't keep 'em if they don't win. Some dogs are winners and some ain't – I say to my trainer, this bloody thing don't win races. Find a buyer. If it's gonna cost me a lot of money I don't want nothing to do with it. And so most of my dogs keep themselves.

'But I like to show a bit of profit, don't I? I like to live out of it, to be quite honest. Me *and* the dogs. I only pay bills out of the bank – I don't draw money out of the bank for me to spend. It comes out of my pot. I mean, if I sell a dog for £1,000, I've got £1,000 in my pocket, ain't I? I don't always show a profit. You have good runs. Sometimes you have one or two little tickles and they come up, then you have a black patch – but I make enough money at it to spend on other things. I have done for a long, long time, yes.

'But then, I've got a lot of information, ain't I? I know there's four or five dogs in my trainer's kennel that are all ripe to win. They're all down in grade. It's been a bit quiet lately, I ain't had a bet for months. The trainer ain't got any money at the moment, and when he ain't got any money, his dogs don't win races. I mean, he's got *money*, but he'll want to have a monkey on, perhaps more than that. He bets that much when he's got a hot one, yes. And the other trainers are doing it as well, of course they are. You just hope to Christ they ain't doing it in the same race you are.'

No wonder those idiots sticking pins in the racecard back just as many winners as I do, I said to Del.

'Well, that is right. I tell you what, if you want to win money punting, to go to the dogs and have a gamble and follow the tipsters, the time to do it is with open races. Trainers don't put dogs in open races and knock 'em out. That's why people like to go open racing. If you go to the dogs like I went to Peterborough, and there was about ten open races, the place was packed. You know you've got sixty triers. If dog tracks ran only open races, there'd be a lot more people there. I mean, the public know it ain't straight, same as they know it about horse racing.

'But when they say, oh, you can't win backing dogs, I think, oh, shut up. They don't know what the hell they're talking about. *They* can't win, I can. My trainer's got forty dogs in his kennels – don't you think I know when there's a tickle on? He doesn't do it with all his owners, of course not. They've got to be people like me – I'm a dog man, ain't I? But he rang up the other day and said, you'd better come tonight. Why, what's happening? He said, — will win tonight. I said, he ain't been picking a leg up. He said, I know. He said, he'll be a big price. Christ, 8/1 we got. That slooshed in.'

I had always known, without knowing how I knew, what went on at the dogs; that behind the apparent bustle and hum was another, more secret level of activity. More precisely, I had always *felt* it. The atmosphere is touching you, silently informing you. Because of it, I could think about the business of the dogs, and words like scams – tickles – coups – stopping – starting – triers – live ones – would begin to ride a merry-go-round in my head; but I had no desire to stop and mount, being happy instead to watch its gaudy whirr. I had no especial need to know, and know *how* I knew, what was going on. The atmosphere, the feeling was enough.

But now, now I can *see* the hand which feeds the mysterious pill, which chalks the informed price; I can *hear* the whisper in the bookmaker's ear, the words of the trainer on the phone to the owner; and all those movements back and forth, from circle of dog men to line of bookmakers, the patterns which they make, I can *read* their significance. I am, in a panoramic kind of way, *in the know*. And now, now that my feeling about the atmosphere of the dogs has been made flesh for me, there is something about this reality that I find strange and elusive. I am fascinated, not so much by the scams, the tickles, the coups, the stopping and starting, but by the way in which these people treat the future: as if it were a concrete entity, something that they can manipulate, slap into shape, sculpt, carve off a bit here, stick on a bit there, as if it were a piece of clay on an armature.

But I do believe that it is in this communion with the future that the real point of gambling lies. This, surely, is the joy of the thing: this feeling of power when the piece of clay on the armature bends to your will, when you know what it will be before it knows itself, when you make of it your own work of art. Is this not the root of pleasure in all gambling? – creating a future, as if it were Galatea, and seeing it come to meet you like a bride? Is this not the feeling that possesses you, when you see the dog that you have appointed a winner, running in first like a herald, signalling the fulfilment of your prophecy? You assert the belief that something will happen: it happens. Such power! The desire for it affects us all. Is gambling on the dogs not, in fact, an extreme and heavily illustrated example of any gamble that you take, of any time in your life when you throw down stakes upon a plan of the future as you wish it to be?

But whatever kind of gambler one is, playing with the

future, the feeling of power that it gives, can be addictive. And the sensation of weakness, of loss, when the future doesn't do what one had gambled that it would, can lead one to gamble all the more in order to recapture the sensation of strength. Unless one has a balanced attitude to the natural to and fro of the feelings of power and weakness, one will, inevitably, lose more than one wins. Dostoevsky: 'One must win at gambling if one can only remain calm and calculating. That's all it is. If one does that, then one cannot lose – one has to win. That's not the problem. But how can the person who knows this secret find the strength and understanding to use it well?'

My father: 'You can't go backing dogs all the time, backing this, and backing that. No, you will lose. That's the trouble with most gamblers: they have too many bets. You've got to be patient. And if you don't win, you don't sit there with your head in your hands saying, "Ooooh, Christ", because you take it over a period of time. You make a few per cent per annum. That's what it's all about.

'But there are gamblers about that are rich one day and penniless the next. I mean there's gamblers and gamblers. It's like all sorts of things you do. Gambling's all right so long as it doesn't affect the way you live – same as drink, same as anything. For some of these men to have £500 on a dog is like me having £50,000 on. £500 of their money could well be their lot. That's what I'm saying. That is how some people gamble.'

And it is surely just a trick of temperament, inexplicable and inescapable, which says that one man will be this kind of gambler, and that the next man will be the other kind of gambler; which designates that one man's plans for the future will be the properly-measured delineations of a master draughtsman, and that the next man's will be the cobbled-together scribblings of a cowboy builder; which says that one man will take pleasure in the feelings of power which arise from successful gambling, and that the next man will be unable to live without them.

A lot of men are in greyhound racing because they are addicted to the idea of being winners. All dog men want to win – as my father says, 'Show me a good loser and I'll show you a fool' – but, for some, winning is all that matters. They are impostor dog men. The difference between the dog man and the impostor dog man can be quite subtle, but it is the attitude towards winning that really sets them apart. The dog man loves to win, but what he really loves is his sport, the vessel that contains both his successes and his failures; winning cannot make him love it more than he already does. He does not have that aggressive hunger, that outward thrusting towards a meal of victory, that immediate need to fill a constant void. Winning comes to him as a smooth and glorious peak which he rides as he glides towards the resigned and familiar plateau.

But it is winning that makes the impostor dog man love his sport. Either as punter or owner, he is gambling, he is throwing down stakes upon the future, but his attitude towards this gambling is somewhat wild and unrealistic. He devours all his successes like a ravenous child, then sicks them up again when he is forced to stomach failures. He wants a life full of peaks, although he doesn't want to have to climb them, and he wants everyone to see him sitting on top of those peaks. All gamblers have a showing off streak in them – Del wants other men to think that he is a wise old bird; Rich the bookmaker wants them to think that he is a bold fellow; John at Harringay wants them to think that he is a man of means – but the impostor dog men are the worse show offs of all, especially those that are owners. My father: 'They'd be happiest if they could get their dogs paraded every night, with them at the head.'

Impostor dog men are often rich men who have come to the sport to buy success in it. They may get their dogs from a breeder, but what they often do is buy them ready-made, as it were, when they are known quantities. To me this seems almost pointless, eliminating as it does so many months of boundless hope, so deep a pride in one's own judgement. The belief of the impostor dog man is that it eliminates also the risk that the greyhound will not be a winner, but this is not necessarily the case.

Del: 'There's a lot of trainers now, they'll buy you what they say is a ready-made champion, but that's no guarantee that it'll turn out to be one. The trainer might get it for you and rip you off. I know someone who paid £10,000 for a greyhound that *just* beat one of my dogs – and I've got nothing that can pick a leg up, not really. There's trainers over here that've got contacts in Ireland. If there's something a bit special over there, news get about, doesn't it? They're there to buy the bugger then. Or they get their agents to buy it. But there are occasions when they pay a lot of money for a dog and it don't come up to scratch. The trainer might get turned over as well. Because a lot of these Irishmen, they get these young dogs and they get up to naughties with 'em, don't they? They give 'em a little bit of help. They run in Ireland and they probably never run as fast again.'

Jerry H*, the man who called Major Brown a drunken old sod, loved the dogs, and loved owning dogs; but only when they were winners. He was wary of his status and didn't feel that he should own anything that might denigrate it. Like a rich man who feels that he must dress the finest wife in the finest clothes, only when he held the finest greyhounds on the end of a lead did he feel himself to be properly attired.

My father: 'He wanted dogs for the wrong reasons. He wanted them so that he could strut about. He used to stand up and sing when his dog was in front. "Keep right on to the end." He used to stand up in the restaurant at Wembley, "Keep – right – on – to – the – end", and everybody would have to get drunk. They'd come from everywhere to that table. All the bloody hangers-on. Used to drive me mad.

'He used to try and buy success. And he'd back dogs that he didn't want to win – that was one of his favourite pastimes. If he didn't like the trainer, or he didn't like the owner, he'd back 'em to try and stop them winning. So that if they lost, he felt he'd won, and if they won – well, he'd forgive 'em then. But he had one great dog and he was always trying to buy another one like him.

'If you've made a few bob it's easier to be flash in dogs than in horses, so that's what they do. They want a champion, they want a bit of glory. Some of these rich men own them and train them – they don't *physically* do it, but they've got the licence, and the kennels are on their premises. That great fat sod that owns —, he's an owner-trainer. Well, he only ran that bitch in the TV

Trophy because he wanted to get on telly. He's always got a story to tell. She ran badly in the final and he's in the paper saying she's only 75 per cent fit. How does he know she's not 72 per cent fit? When a man says a dog's 75 per cent fit you start wondering what he gets up to in the feed bowl. I mean, normal trainers make up a bathful of bread, a bathful of vegetables, and they mince up a load of meat and that's it. But when a man's only got a few dogs, you can bet he's got his missus cooking up some little titbit for 'em. A dog's a dog, it's not a bloody Caprice eater.

'This man sounds like he leaves the races in the bloody paper. I used to have a trainer like that. He'd be talking to one and all, and rubbing the dog down, and this, that and the other – he couldn't keep his hands off the bloody dog if it was in a final. And he'd transmit all his nerves to it. This man says the bitch was dehydrated – he might be one of those lunatics that doesn't believe in giving it water. The bloody comedians that own dogs. How does he know she's dehydrated? What, did she tell him? She's a dodgy little cow probably. You don't know what they get up to – they get up to all manner of things, some of these people. He's probably been galloping her all week because she was only 72 per cent fit.'

My father has real scorn for those who try to become dog men and remain resolutely unable to acquire the necessary nous; who remain impostor dog men. 'It's no good going into dog racing and thinking you're going to win, that's crazy. Christ, I've seen it happen so many times.'

The background of the vast majority of greyhound owners is one in which the most natural thing in the world was to go to the dogs. They have grown up with the sport, and they have not grown away from it. My father: 'Most of them, really, are working class that have made some money. Not all of them; it attracts other types of people, but really it's a working man's sport. It's the masses that make sport, isn't it? I mean, even a sport like horse racing, which is full of moneyed people – there's still a lot of people pay to go the tracks, aren't there? The only difference between horse racing and dog racing, in my book – I mean, there's as big bloody low lifers at the horses as at the dogs – the only difference is in the people that own. They're a different class of people, on the whole.

'But most people who own dogs have got a few quid. You can tell by the cars that drive up to the kennels on Sunday mornings. There's Mercedes, and there's this and that – and they're probably businessmen. There aren't many people own dogs if they've got no money, unless a few of them club together. '"Who owns that dog", I say to my trainer, "he ain't a bad dog?" "Well, there's a couple of old boys got it, and I think the Dad's got a share in it . . ." Down at the kennels you see the old lary boys, that as soon as you see them you can tell they're dog men, and they'll stand there in a group, three or four of them, looking at one dog.'

Which is why the true dog man, who loves his sport, who knows that owning a greyhound brings that love very close to him, but who knows that he cannot compete in a world in which that greyhound could cost him a year's wages, will spurn the licensed stadia and take his love to the flapping tracks. When this man owns his flapping dog, then he owns his sport. He is the descendant of the proud, self-sufficient dog man who walked the grimy northern streets with his delicate whippet at his side. In the makeshift arenas that hold all that he needs – the dogs, the race, the bet – and nothing that he does not – the restaurants, the television screens, the razzmatazz – he can feel his own identity: can feel it subsumed into the power of his sport, but can feel it also separate, defined, acknowledged. Of course there are two sports going on at the flaps: the sport of greyhound racing, and the sport of trying to work out what's going on behind the greyhound racing. Of course flapping lacks controls and regulations. Of course there are continual coups and scams and tickles afoot, of course there are races in which all the owners get together to back one dog and dope the other five, of course there are changeling dogs, running under one name, performing under another. Of course, as my father says, 'You get all the little naughties that you get in every walk of life, who think they're the clever boys.' Of course the true dog man will be abreast of all this and possibly in on some of it. But *his* greyhound will not be.

'He's a one-dog man and it's a household pet. And that tries every time it runs. Anybody could have a little dog and run it at the flaps. That's their pride and joy. They save their money up and they might ring my trainer, or someone like him, and say, "I want a good dog. I want a good dog to run at so-and-so." "Well, I've got one here, it'll cost you fifteen hundred quid, or a thousand quid." But they'll win that back if it's a good dog. Up North, and in Scotland, it goes on all the time. I mean, they ring up my trainer and tell him, "Cor, what a great dog you sent me." It's burning the track up and the bloke's elated about it, he's the king of the place – and it's only a fair dog down here: A4, A5 – up in the flaps you've got a bloody champion. Flapping's not completely crooked because some people won't touch a hair of their dog's head. They want it to run its best; they're proud of it.

'Most of the dogs that leave me are better off away from me. They're treated like she is,' said my father, touching with his toe our mongrel bitch. 'That's where a lot of my dogs go. That's where I like them to go. They sleep on the sofa, and they stay on the sofa until they die.'

7

The Dog Man and his Boy

It is the dogs themselves that keep the very heart of the sport pure. Yes, gambling is what it's all about, and the men who sit in betting shops all day, frowning with the ecstatic pain of self-imposed martyrdom over *The Greyhound Life*, might just as well be picking out mechanical toys for all they care about the animals that win and lose for them; but compared with the desperate grubby glamour of casino gambling, say, there is a soft and secret innocence within the world of greyhound racing. It's well hidden, to be sure. It is unseen by most observers, and it would be denied by most participants; men who go greyhound racing pride themselves on their self-containment. The flame of love that burns inside them for the dogs, this love they hug within, feeding it only by giving out bits of themselves – jokes, would-be shrewd sidelong glances, £20 notes. It would be betrayed if they gave more, if they despaired or rejoiced too wildly over money won or lost, if they showed emotion.

It is a love of gambling for its own sake. But it is something more. The gambling fulfils a desire within the dog men, a whole reckless world inside their zipped-up bodies; a world which never changes in its

160

constant changeability, which never moves as it races. But the bond between the dog men and the dogs fulfils another dimension of desire. It touches their human heart.

I learned this first not through greyhounds, but through horses, which have the same capacity to touch those who gamble upon them, although it is more difficult for them to do so: too remote, too expensive, too tall, too splendid, surrounded too thoroughly by a society of impregnable, richly neighing horse men. Anyway, this was Boxing Day 1990, and I was at Milton Keynes dog track with my father, where the prevailing winds of amiable cynicism which breathe through dog racing were being met by a counterbreeze of amiable cynicism away from Christmas. '*She* likes it . . . the kids liked it . . . we had a bit of a bull and a cow . . . got through it all right . . . not sorry it's over . . .' The innocence that Christmas Day can still reveal in people was being deftly masked by the social smell of beer, the social fug of cigarettes, the jovial toughness of the battle with the bookmakers, the sound of horse racing on the television – for these dog men were not just fleeing the pressure to be sociable in their own homes to order to bet on dogs. No indeed, they had made several telephone calls that morning of an urgent, private nature, and they had money riding on the horses. Boxing Day is one of the biggest racing days of the year. The biggest meeting of the day is Kempton, the biggest race at Kempton is the King George VI Chase, and that year the biggest horse of them all, Desert Orchid, the Mick the Miller of our age, was attempting to win the King George VI for the fourth time. But so cynical were some of the dog men that they had even bet against him, that was how cynical they were.

Which makes it odd that when the race was underway and the dog men were pretending to have only a passing interest in it – pretending to study the form, pretending to order a round, pretending to watch the parade of greyhounds around the track – there should have come from them so powerful a surge of reluctant love, of feelings repressed on the previous day, or on any other day. From out of the chinks in their gruff, embarrassed armour came the little asides: 'Over you go son'; 'That's it feller'; a gradual angling of the body towards the television, a childlike smile, a softening recognition within these men that they would rather see the realisation of something magical, rather have the memory of this horse's victory than reap the rewards of his defeat. When the race was over, the dog men blinked at the sentient head of the grey horse, as it inclined with wise, quiescent nods towards the love of the crowd – 'Glad the old boy won it' – and then returned to their external selves, buttoning up their dishevelled emotions as they went.

That's what crowds must have been like with Mick the Miller. When the 1931 Derby was rerun they must have been willing him to make the impossible possible, to show that he was not an exhausted dog of nearly five but a creature running on the magical fuels of myth. Partly this is a selfish desire to feel that one is helping to create the myth oneself. There is also simple enjoyment of partaking of and adding to a communal emotion. But there is love there too, unconditional and pure and the kind that it is very difficult to give to adult human beings.

Of course Mick was unusual. He pierced the hearts of even the most hardened gamblers – they felt that they knew him, you see. Of course the degree to which the dogs engage with the love of those that follow them varies enormously. It varies with different dogs and with different men. But I have never met a true dog man who did not yearn towards those beautiful greyhounds, conceal this as he might beneath camel coat or suede blouson.

Every true dog man will want to own a dog and bring his love closer to him. If he does own, as like as not you will see him at his trainer's kennels on a Sunday, pub face cramped with joviality, leisure clothes as pronounced as billboards, interspersing the dog talk with a bit of chat about his haulage company or his furniture warehouse as he absently fondles the ears of the greyhound he has come to see. On the back seat of his BMW is a box of dog biscuits; on its bonnet there may well be a small silver greyhound. I met a man who, every week, visited a bitch that he had paid to keep at the kennels for the ten years or so since she had stopped racing. Her ribs showed like bars on an electric fire, her back was humped, there was nothing left of her face but eyes and she walked uncertainly, as if on stilts. She was too tired and weakened to show joy at the approach of her owner, but one could see it in the slow lengthening and relaxation of the lines of her head. As the man talked dog talk, he held her salty muzzle in place at his hip. The bitch stood beside him, perfectly still within the helpless quivering of her body, receiving the gently rhythmic touch of affection.

Although this scene stopped me going to the kennels

for a while – I simply couldn't bear to watch as everything about the dog declined except her love and trust – writing this book has meant that I would start visiting again. On perhaps the first of these visits, I learned that the bitch had died. The tiny space that opened inside my heart was nothing compared with how I would have felt had I seen her every week; of necessity there are gaps in one's dealings with greyhounds. Better just to learn that they have died. Better not to think about it at all.

It is dangerous to get too fond of them. I was able to put years between my memories and myself with dogs like Commutering and London Lights, to put them into another dimension, turn them into symbols of my childhood, but the dogs we own now, the Jerpoint dogs, I may live with forever: Jerpoint Daley, wildly lovable, pinning his paws to your shoulders like a rampant dance partner; Jerpoint Joey, gazing up at you in touching submission; Jerpoint Ali, my secret favourite, relentlessly greedy, her hindquarters bustling like a little housewife's as she walks along beside you. And the litter of pups that came over from Ireland: my father had high hopes of these, which by the time this book comes out will have been either satisfied or shattered. There were two black-and-white males, one of them a real and almost conscious beauty, already standing calm and still and confident, as if on a winner's rostrum. There was a wild and rumbustious dark brindle with a triangular, reptile head. There was a fascinatingly huge and skinny black bitch with the long back, predatory legs, loping tread and hanging head of a wolf. There was a smaller, prettier bitch and a quieter, honey brindle dog, who trotted at your side with his head in the air, like a thin and tiny horse.

We visited them when they had just arrived. I looked
at them, and instantly sealed my ineluctable bond; my
father, hiding his pleasure at the sight of them cavorting
round their pens, watched and gave out sidelong pro-
nouncements. His sole caveat – normally he'd have had
too many to bother voicing them – was that the dark
brindle seemed to have a dodgy back foot that he threw
sideways when he ran. I couldn't see what my father
meant; I thought that he was trying to counterbalance
the casual stretch of his hand towards the eager muzzles.

We stood and watched as they performed for us. Very
new, they seemed to me, their limbs still slightly slippery, their coats still soft and loose; a little panicky in
their changed circumstance, but because they were so
young this was translating itself into an extreme energy
and an artless desire to please. As we looked at them –
so young, so new, so eager – the air seemed to swell with
the infinity of possibility. In that moment, those dogs
could have been anything.

And then, of course, they started trialling, the future
became the present and the dream dogs became six out
of thousands of working greyhounds. My father rang to
tell me how they'd run. 'That big, good-looking one, he
graded. The black bitch, she walked out of the traps,
had a look around and then flew. She'd have graded if
she'd have known what she was doing. She started running like hell after she crossed the line. The other bitch
is in season. That other black-and-white dog graded –
he went all right, he's got a bit of early. But in fact the
little one, that weed, the brindle, now he went the best of
the lot.'

'What about the big brindle?'

'He's throwing that foot a bit. He ran terribly wide. He didn't grade, oh Christ no. He might be all right next time.'

But at the next trial – when all the others graded – the big brindle was again splaying the back foot that my father had remarked on at our first, idyllic viewing. 'I don't think he's going to be much good. He ran off the track, poor little bugger.'

And then I thought of him skidding round the pen, his back bunched and springy, life shimmering out from between his ribs, the stripes of his tiger coat converged into a dark, feral, vital and very male mass. He had been the most confident of the six pups. I had thrown him a biscuit and he had gone instantly, absolutely wild: he hadn't realised that he was meant to eat it and had chased it instead, tossing it into the air with his nose and trying like a footballer to subdue it between his feet. Perhaps he had wanted to kill it before he could eat it. Eventually, he did launch it into his throat and then, after a violent bit of crunching, he stuck his tiger snake head out at me – making a hole in the fence of the pen – and demanded more biscuits and more, much more attention. He knew beyond a doubt that he would get both.

I wondered if it would have seemed more fitting if my father had said that the other brindle, the small one that lay on the ground when you tried to stroke him, was going to be no good. He had seemed so helpless, an accepter of his fate. Yet he had been saved by his ability. He was going to be all right. Instead, it was the unconscious life force, the strong, the fearless, who had been betrayed by a weakness about which nothing could be done. Accumulating and expending vitality in perfect rhythm, sharpening and readying his atavistic instincts, fighting mad to do the job for which he had been bred and prepared, he was all unaware that he was unfit to do it.

My father told me that the dog might run round tracks with banked bends, which might accommodate his dodgy foot. I left it at that. I would assume that yes, he would be able to run round tracks with banked bends. If he couldn't, how could I bear to know about it? I would never erase the memory of his tiger snake spirallings, the dark virile look of him on that summery Sunday morning, when he could have been another Commutering, or better than another Commutering. I couldn't be forced to connect that memory with the knowledge of his decline thereafter.

This had forcibly reminded me of how impossible it is to get too close to these dogs. It is, perforce, a strange emotion that the dog man has for his greyhounds, a mixture of toughness and tenderness, of fascination and detachment. The proportions differ – as my father says, 'There are professional and there are amateur owners' – but the mixture is always the same. If you are to be a dog man who in any way deserves the name, it cannot be otherwise.

My father is so much a dog man that he talks about human runners as if they were greyhounds. 'What trap's Linford in?' he will ask before a race. Conversely he talks about greyhounds as if they were people. This is typical of a dog man. One of the essentials of dog talk is the attribution of characteristics to dogs that might help to make sense of the mysteries, and make predictable that arbitrariness, of greyhound racing. The idea that a dog runs without knowing what it is doing cannot be countenanced by a dog man.

My father: 'You can have two greyhounds – if you clock them they're within hundredths of a second of each other, they're almost equal, and from the trap to the line they could be the same. But one of them will win three times as many races as the other one. And you don't know why. It's inside, you see.'

'Inside' – the character of a greyhound – is, in fact, the mystery at the heart of dog racing; a mystery which the dog men will never stop trying to fathom. They can attempt to manipulate the future, and they can believe every time they do so that they will succeed, that they will make of its murkiness something crystal and sure; but the truth is that they can never do the thing that they are really trying to do. The dog men cannot control the dogs. They cannot make it, they cannot make *them*, their trophy. They will always be at the mercy of two mysteries: the mystery of luck, and the mystery of the greyhound, the dog which they can own but cannot rule.

Certainly, trainers don't have the control over the future of the dogs that they think they have, simply because very few greyhounds run every race in the same way. They do not always run to win. They do not always try their hardest to pass other dogs and, if they have the lead, they do not always try to stay there. This is the characteristic which led Paddy Sweeney, a vet and one of the most knowledgeable of dog men, to say that 90 per cent of greyhounds were not 'honest'. He then went on to ask, indeed, why should they be? No human desire for glory, no jockey on their backs, nothing except that instinct to make them chase and that breeding to make them track. Only in a few greyhounds is there something that makes them want to win every single time they run. To see this determination being pulled out of a dog is as uplifting as to see it being wrung from a human athlete.

These are the great-hearted dogs, and they are the ones that every dog man wants to own. The finest of them will, like Mick the Miller, have brains as well as heart; but if one had to choose between the clever greyhound – which knows how to negotiate a track, how to see gaps and go for them, how to wait for other dogs to go in order to give himself space, how far to let them go before starting to catch up with them again – and the stupid greyhound – which tries to get to the rail when there are five dogs between him and it, but which tries to do this foolish thing with all his might – then one would choose the great-hearted idiot dog. A greyhound that runs every time to win is a greyhound to treasure.

If a dog is too clever it may, in fact, lose heart. It may get bored. It may even clock that it is never going to catch that bloody hare. Then, as my father puts it, it will 'fall out of love with racing'. Most greyhounds are so intensely bred to run around a track that they will carry on doing so even if the hare stops, but the very intelligent ones have minds of their own.

A dog may also lose heart if it has been hurt. Depending on the shape of the track, the first bend, into which greyhounds launch themselves like missiles, will almost always occasion either a minor ruck or a disastrous collision; it is scarcely possible that it should not do so. Only luck and a very good racing manager will get those six dogs running smoothly around that sudden curve. It has to be planned like a military strategy: the three dog gets out fastest; the one dog is fairly quick; the six sometimes breaks, sometimes doesn't, but it runs so wide it won't get in anything else's way; the five doesn't get out but has pace to the bend and *might* try to cut across to the rails, which it will be able to do because the three will have gone straight into the lead; the two won't start running until it gets into the back straight, and the four is a useless old scrubber. So round the bend they should go in an orderly procession: three at the head, one and possibly five just behind on its inside, two and four side by side at the back and six somewhere out towards the carpark. No ruck, no collision.

Except that dogs don't always do what you think they're going to do. I can barely recall a race in which there was no push or shove of some kind at the first bend, and usually somewhere else round the track as well. Races are not just won on speed, they are won on tactics, conscious or subconscious. Some tracks create more trouble than others (Wimbledon, for example, is terrible: its bends are so vicious, and make races so unpredictable, that many people think the Derby should not be run there.) Mostly there are just skirmishes, but in a four-bend race they will effectively ruin the chance of at least one dog. And I have seen greyhounds tossed into the air or knocked sideways by the force with which they hit another dog. It is frightening to watch and it is surely frightening to do, however wildly a dog is transported by desire. My father: 'Oh they're brave, they're brave, they're not without courage. Greyhounds are a brave dog. And a noble dog, in my opinion.'

Usually they carry on running after these fatal-looking skids and ricochets, but there is always a terrible moment when they might not. The crash will probably not have killed them, but the shattered leg may be irreparable. My father once owned a tiny bitch, 50lb or so but brave beyond her size, who tried to impose her will on the first bend by hurling herself at 75lb dogs, commanding them with all her meagre strength to make room for her. They simply threw her away as if she were a rubbish bag being flung on a dump cart. We watched this happen and for an instant everything stopped. Then I started wailing, my father started frowning and – luck was with her – the little dog started running. Several seconds after the race was over, she completed her own race like a lioness, like a warrior.

But she was never quite the same again. 'No, she lost her bottle then.' Most greyhounds become more careful as they get older, having to some degree suffered bumps and scuffles, and gaps that they might previously have gone for they back away from instead. But some of them have always been cautious. 'Like little Ali. I thought she was a dodgy cow, you know, but she isn't. She's very careful. I mean, she should have beaten that bitch the other night in that final at Oxford. She had the legs of it, but she wouldn't go through with it on the bends. She caught her, but instead of finishing the job she thought, oh, I don't know, perhaps I haven't got room, type of thing, you know. But if she'd gone through with it on the rail she'd have got the lead and then she would have won it.'

This is not exactly 'dishonesty' in Ali; it is simply that her intelligence sometimes outweighs her desire. But the effect is still that she doesn't always run to win. Dishonesty in dogs varies in degree, of course, as with human beings. There are *really* dishonest greyhounds, which are not interested in the hare at all. They are following the other dogs, sometimes in the hope of having a little nip out of one of them, and if they get away from them and run into the lead, they often stop trying out of boredom. But most dogs simply don't always run to win. You can't know whether or not they are going to do it, and you can't know why they do it; it may be, as a dog man said to me in the pub after the kennels one Sunday, that 'When we say they're not trying, it's like, some days you might look all right, but you don't feel 100 per cent, know what I mean? They're only like human beings. And most people've got something a little bit dodgy in 'em, ain't they? You don't know what it is or where it is, but it's like, sometimes you get drunk and you're the life and soul of the party and everybody wants to know you, and then the next time you're a bloody nuisance to one and all.'

But whatever is behind it, the 'dishonesty' factor is a real swine to have to contend with on top of all the other variables. You might think that you have a race as sussed as is possible: 'That has got to lead to the first bend', you will have grindingly concluded, 'and if it makes the bend in front then *there is no way* it won't win' – and then the dog that you have selected, the dog that cannot lose, will have an off night, will run dishonestly, and will lollop in fourth with an almost sadistic glint in its eye. You will blame the trainer: 'That bastard', you will say, 'he knocked it out' – but in fact the blame will lie with the dog. It knocked itself out. A few years ago, my father and his partner Roy owned a dog called Jerpoint Diamond, who still holds the track record at Milton Keynes, so freakish was his time. He was probably the best dog my father ever had, faster than Commutering. But Diamond didn't always run to win, and Commutering had been one of the rare, great-hearted dogs.

My father: 'Some of them have got hearts the size of walnuts. Hazelnuts, some of 'em. Peanuts. And sometimes – I remember one of my old trainers had a little dog in his kennel many years ago. It was a real weed, you know. And that was a great greyhound. And he was running it and I said, "You know, you could win the Derby with that dog if you didn't run the guts out of it." And he would've won the Derby with it. He didn't win it because the bloody dog was tired out . . . But by Christ that could run. That little dog, he'd run his heart out.

'But it was a freak, you see. It wasn't much outside, but it was good inside. Now Diamond was good outside, and not terribly good inside. He had a fine physique, and he had quality about him, but he wasn't always 100 per cent. He used to be tailed off last and go like hell and win, and then another time he'd lead and lose, which you couldn't believe. All according what sort of mood he was in. He won two Summer Cups at Milton Keynes. In one of the heats he let this bitch come and beat him, and then in the final she was leading and he gave her a bloody running lesson. He ran when he felt like it. And there's nothing much a trainer can do about it, if the dog's a dog of moods.'

Ah, the pleasure of knowledge, the difference it can make to the way in which one sees things. Not being a true dog person, I should never have been able to analyse the racing character of Jerpoint Diamond; but once it had been explained to me, how fascinating it was to watch him run. We have a video of all his races. I watched it both before and after I had discussed the dog with my father, and the subsequent sharpening of my perceptions was extremely satisfying. Yet if only I were able to work it out for myself! But I cannot do that. I find it easier to be fanciful than knowledgeable about my sport.

Diamond was a big, staggeringly handsome dog, with a white coat patched with brindle. His running style was dramatic. To see him lengths behind the leader; to see him in hopeless positions; to see him suddenly decide that now was the time to move; to see him disappear into a crowd of dogs and then to see him – was it him? the split second's agony of distinguishing the jacket . . . yes him – to see his snowy body emerge disdainful and cool and hugely superior, and to know that this was *our* dog, *our* boy . . . Even now, five years on from his running years, there is a real and ridiculous pride in watching the video of his victories. There is, too, a real chagrin in watching the races that he could have won but gave up on instead – although in a way I admire him for it. Why the hell shouldn't he have had a night off if he chose? I'm sure that I'd be like that if I were a greyhound – the sling-it-in, sod-you, bolshie type.

Diamond won the Scottish St Leger but, to me, his most exciting win was the Ballyregan Bob Stakes at Wembley, a 655-metre race inaugurated to honour what was certainly the best greyhound of the 1980s, and possibly the best of all time. It was not so much the victory which thrilled me – unusually for him, Diamond led all the way and won with unchallenged ease – more the sight of our dog standing on the winner's rostrum next to Ballyregan Bob: two nonchalant stars, two colleagues in celebrity. At the age of five, Bob was already grey about the muzzle and looked far less beautiful than the buoyant young Diamond, but his ears were still flickering up and down like flames and he carried his fame with conscious dignity. Of course Diamond was not so great a greyhound, but standing there next to Bob like a glamorous dauphin, one saw that he was worthy of the same respect, that he was in the same pre-eminent sphere. It actually made one proud to have known him.

I understood something about the relationship between the dog man and his boy when I watched Diamond standing on that rostrum. Watching him, newly flush with achievement, I had a sudden surge of yearning for the feel of victory; and of course, what I really wanted was for it to be *me* that was standing there. But sport allows his followers to be victorious even if they are not victors. *They* may not be winners, but they can pick winners, or support winners, or – best of all – own winners. Even if I cannot stand there myself, there is something very sweet in seeing my greyhound on the rostrum in my place, in standing beside him and beneath him, with the pride that I feel in victory blossoming above a thin and distant pain, that I can never inhabit this victory, can never feel it quite as wholly as I would wish.

The St Leger is greyhound racing's second most important prize: only the Derby can induce stronger pride and pain in a winning owner. Jerpoint Diamond was even money favourite for the 1988 St Leger and, after more than twenty years' involvement with top class racing, it seemed that my father was finally about to win a classic. I didn't know then that Diamond was a dog of moods and I had swanned into Wembley entirely prepared to go down and help pick up the trophy. It was an autumn evening of high bathos. For the first two hours my father, Roy and (to a lesser extent) I were treated like celebrities. We stood in the centre of a circle of jittery dog talk, of arabesques of hilarity which rose like soufflés and whinnied nervously down again, of surges of certainty in which the dog had already won the race, of thuds of sobriety in which we remembered that the race had not yet been run. Pat, the breeder of all the Jerpoint greyhounds, had come over from Ireland, accompanied by members of his family. Bottles of champagne lurked like flashers.

The whole build-up was acutely, excruciatingly, hysterically enjoyable. God only knows how I would handle it now, involved as I am in the dog world again; at the time the race had come upon me as if from nowhere, as a wonderful surprise, but even so I was a laughing wreck by the time it was about to be run. I stepped out into the black night, face brightly fixed, thoughts skittering round my brain as if in a maze. I was praying as the hare began its circuit, but with no apparent purpose, rather as if I had been hypnotised to do so.

The race itself was anticlimactic to the point of comedy. Diamond started indifferently, moved into an indifferent middle phase and, with a burst of supreme indifference, finished in the fourth position that he had steadily maintained. I couldn't believe that was it. Forty seconds of meaninglessness. Right, I thought, that was fine, now let's have another go, shall we? But I was walking back to the bar; I knew really that it was over. What a night for a dog of moods to have a mood. You sod, I screamed silently at him from behind my good sportswoman smiles, that was the St Leger final, how dare you treat it as if it were a £100 race at Milton Keynes? It was the closest I have ever come to hating a greyhound. I didn't know the dog, you see, otherwise I couldn't have thought of disliking him. What I was feeling was a shadow of the emotion that suffuses losing gamblers who have merely backed a number. They are not true dog men.

Some of the dog men back in the owners' bar had, by now, forgotten just why the celebrities were supposed to be famous. The celebrities themselves were resigned to a life of obscurity, whose start they were heralding with half pints of lager. A few kind dog people stood by, in desultory attitudes very different from the tight, soldierly rings that they had made around us ten minutes earlier, keeping up a sympathetic silence, minimally interspersed with driblets of stoic philosophy. 'Ne'er mind.' 'Coo dear, oh dear, oh dear.' 'What a bloody thing, eh?' 'Can't believe it, can ya?' I had to stop looking at them because every time I caught one of their eyes I got from them a sorrowing cross between a smile, a shrug and a tut, and I felt that it must be wearying for them to have to keep doing it. My father looked as though he had thought this would happen all along. Roy looked as though he was only being held together by his smile. Together they watched the replay on the television screen and tried to make sense of Diamond's nonsense run.

Losing a classic final is always miserable (we had gone through it before, with the Grand National and the

Cesarewitch), because you always believe, deep down, that your dog is going to run a scenario rather than a race. But losing when you are hot favourite, and when your dog decides on a whim to run like a pig, is quite gruesome. After your own disbelief wears off, you begin to realise that your dog's failure is reverberating through the stadium. You begin to hear the griping and to feel the vibes. You divine that some of the dog men who had been pressing round you earlier had had a lot of money riding ante-post on your greyhound. About half an hour after the St Leger final, my father and I slid away from the bar like lizards; by then I was feeling a weight of irrational guilt on top of my phlegmatic chagrin.

My father: 'Diamond lost his reputation, really, through his inconsistent running. The only time to back him was when he was 6/1, 8/1, 10/1. Then he always used to win. If you had him at even money, the bugger never put it in. But he could run.'

My father has been lucky, in that he has had some terrific greyhounds; but he has also been unlucky, in that he hasn't won as much with them as he should have done. Commutering was as good as any St Leger dog around at the time; After the Show was a middle distance dog who could have won the Gold Collar. Their dam, No Mabel, then threw an outstanding litter by Monalee Champion (possibly the best stud dog of the last twenty years), whose king and queen were Chain Gang and Pitman's Brief, a black satin double act that shimmered with class. Chain Gang's conformation was so fine that he was even used as a mannequin when Harringay had him model the eponymous coat for their Golden Jacket open, a race which he failed to win. He

did, however, win the most beautiful trophy in greyhound racing, the Regency.

My father and Frank Melville* had gone down to
Brighton for the meeting as guests of a man who owned
another finalist in the race. This man was so sure that he
was going to win, and so sorry for my father about this,
that he decided he would buy dinner for him and Frank
as compensation. 'We were his guests, and we duffed
him up.' Midway through dinner, Chain Gang swooped
away with the race, and my father left the table to go and
get the prize. The host ordered champagne and powerfully insisted that he would still buy the dinner; my
father and Frank tried desperately to be sober and sympathetic and conceal their hysterical happiness; while
sitting at the table with them all, a vast and unignorable
presence, was the huge sculpted figure of Mercury, flying beside two big greyhounds, which comprised the
silver enormity of the Regency Trophy.

After this triumph, Chain Gang and his sister both
reached the final of the Cesarewitch, the marathon classic held at Belle Vue. What happened on this occasion
was actually worse than the non-event of the 1988 St
Leger. Both greyhounds were heavily fancied and one of
them, it seemed, was surely bound to win. Instead of
which they collided with each other.

'One of them tried to pinch the rail off the other one. I
remember sitting there with Frank and saying, "Oh,
Christ, I know what's going to happen now." *And* it did.
She came up to Chain Gang, trying to get to the rail, and
she ran into the back of him. Frank said, "Bloody bitch."
I said, "Frank, if she'd have got through on the rail,
she'd have won it. She was catching him hand over fist.

What was she going to do when she passed him, stop dead?" Because when she put her acceleration in, she was arguably a better dog than he was. But he was out in front and gone, and if *she* hadn't been in the race then *he'd* have won it. They did each other.

'She was favourite to win it. She held the track record at Catford for a long time over 1000 yards – as she got older she ran further. That happens to bitches. But she was a cow. She wouldn't go past anything on the outside. I mean, why run in the back of a dog trying to get to the rail when there isn't space? All that breed did it. Chain Gang'd have done it to her. But he was a better tracker than she was. She was a clumsy cow. Because she was a beautiful looking bitch, class oozing out of her – well, they both had. She was the best looking bitch I ever had, oh, she was a beautiful bitch. But she never gave of her best, really.'

Pitman's Brief and Chain Gang were great-hearted greyhounds: they ran to win. No Mabel almost always threw genuine dogs. But their flaw was a kind of stubbornness. They *would not* abandon their desire to run on the inside of the track. It is impossible to know why – did it make them feel more secure? – and it was certainly impossible to do anything about it. It was part of their mysterious characters.

'Now a good greyhound, my idea of a proper greyhound, a great tracker, will lead all the way, and he'll come from behind, and he'll run on the inside, and he'll run on the outside, and he'll run out of any trap. And there's very few of them about. And really, most of them that are like that are so far superior anyway, their pace makes it easy for them – like Ballyregan Bob.'

*

Ballyregan Bob, the dog that won thirty-two races in succession in the mid-1980s, breaking a record that had been set in 1979 by an American greyhound named Joe Dump, who won thirty-one races on his local track in Alabama, was as close as one might come to the definition of a perfect greyhound. To look at him is to see and feel no doubt. In his eyes is the near blankness of absolute brilliance. It is the look that one sees in certain athletes when they know that they have entered their unassailable prime, and that the only thing they are running against is themselves. Their eyes are indifferent to any other competitor because they are inhabiting a sphere of their own. Scurlogue Champ, on the other hand, Ballyregan Bob's great and only rival, was more freakish than perfect. Bob's trainer, George Curtis, described him as 'the most exciting greyhound I have ever seen'. Infertile, constantly injured, of oddly self-effacing appearance and with the most peculiar running style of any dog in the history of the sport, he seemed scarcely like a greyhound at all, more a phenomenon without precedent.

My father: 'He didn't chase. He ran a whole circuit of the track sometimes before he'd chase. He ran with his head in the air. It seemed like he knew what he was doing – "I'll let the silly buggers go, then I'll get started." I can remember the first time I saw him run, I think it was at Harringay, and Frank said, "Now this is some sort of dog." Dogs I've had, good dogs, have been paceless compared with him. He had a freakish turn of foot.'

I never saw Scurlogue Champ run, and I regret it. He was seen one night by a journalist who said that 'if greyhound racing was always like this, you'd never keep it off the telly'. The sight of him storming through to win from maybe twenty lengths behind the fifth greyhound must have been sport at its best: that which induces a sense that the physically impossible is, in fact, possible. The dog won fifty-one out of sixty-three races and broke twenty track records. Ballyregan Bob won forty-two out of forty-eight races and broke sixteen track records.

The feats of these two greyhounds, made possible by their superordinate speed, are unparalleled in the history of the sport. Not even Mick the Miller reigned with such effortless supremacy. They were so much faster than any other dog around that they could either win their races by huge distances or by gathering vast amounts of lost ground between their peerless feet. It is hard to think of any human athlete of comparable superiority. There isn't one; you can only say that these dogs were running like Coe and Ovett in a world still running like Roger Bannister. There have been great greyhounds before, but none so disdainful as these two of all opposition.

Scurlogue Champ is the unfathomable one. Ballyregan Bob was simply great; but Scurlogue was mysteriously so. When I think of him, I imagine a mythical dog, whose body is inhabited by the spirit of a careless, laughing god; a god so protected by its own superiority that its greatest delight is to play games with it. For it is quite amazing that a dog of such extraordinary pace should also be a dog of such extraordinary character, that he should be freakish in every way. He is the sort of creature that gets invented, not the sort that exists. And of course the fact that he was infertile strengthens my fancy. He has probably impregnated some caged Irish bitch in the form of a shower of gold – except that nothing quite like Scurlogue Champ has ever appeared since, or indeed before.

Injuries punctuated his career, frustrated his followers, made more precious his appearances and, again appropriately to the myth, protected him from having to contest the race against Ballyregan Bob: it was fitting to the image of both dogs that neither should have beaten the other. But although Scurlogue's injuries heightened his mystery – there he was, yet again, being carried off the track like a young, battle-wounded emperor – these can be rationally explained. Ballyregan Bob was also frequently injured. Those strains and pulls and tears of the muscles were in fact the symptoms of the dogs' greatness.

For these two represented an ideal in the science of greyhound breeding. They were physical embodiments of an apex reached, and so lofty, so etiolated, so precarious was that apex that it all but toppled over into the rocky seas of overbreeding. So fine-tuned were the nerves and sinews of these dogs that they constantly collapsed and snapped beneath their ordinary workload. Scurlogue Champ and Ballyregan Bob were, in fact, almost too well-bred to do the thing that they had been bred to do.

My father: 'Ever since the day go, the breeding's improved, hasn't it? A dog like Mick the Miller, that was invincible, that stood out alone, he wouldn't win the first race at Milton Keynes tonight. That's why there's many more injuries. The greyhound's frame hasn't changed – lightened up a bit if anything – but the speed . . . it's arguable that they run about eight miles an hour faster than they used to.' And this is how you have these dogs who, for all their meaty horseshoe of a backside and strong columnar shoulders, still look frighteningly fragile with their brittle legs, their knobbly feet, their eyes that gleam at the hilt of their stiletto faces like huge, black tears; these dogs, whose primitive instincts send them hurtling towards a bend which their perfected breeding ensures that they will reach at nearly forty miles an hour.

Scurlogue Champ and Ballyregan Bob ran at speeds which may not be surpassed for many years, or indeed ever. But they won very few of the recognised big races. The only classic that they have between them is Scurlogue's 1985 Cesarewitch, and his only other big race wins were the '85 and '86 Television Trophies; Ballyregan Bob's most prestigious win was the 1985 Essex Vase at Romford. Their most famous triumphs usually came in sponsored races that had been set up for them: Scurlogue's 'Champ Comes to Glasgow Stakes' at Shawfield (where, such was the dog's glamour, the meeting was an all-ticket event); or the 'John Power Show Down' at Wembley. This is typical of the age, which, instead of allowing the two greyhounds to triumph within the established sphere of their sport, created spheres for them. They were stars and they were going to be protected; they were going to have little worlds built for them, they were not going to be risked in somebody else's. And they were not going to race each other until there was nothing else left for them to do.

They were, in human terms, world record holders rather than Olympic gold medallists. Certainly with Ballyregan Bob, one gets the feeling that the record of

32 consecutive wins was the aim, rather than the Derby
or the St Leger, both of which he was entirely capable of
winning. That record is so remarkable that one understands perfectly the care that was taken with the dog; the
days when Mick the Miller could almost incidentally win
nineteen races on the trot are long gone. But the slight
air of calculation, and of operating in another sphere
from that of other greyhounds, which clings to the
careers of Ballyregan Bob and Scurlogue Champ, means
that although they may be the greatest dogs of all time,
they may not be remembered with *quite* that mixture of
sentimental worship and judicious awe that signifies, for
the dog men, the highest possible regard. Of course,
when they were running, they were the centrepieces of
the whole sport. The wild men on the terraces screamed
for Scurlogue as he pumped them high with displaced
adrenalin; the dog world shuddered with pleasure as it
watched Bob walk the tightrope toward his thirty-second
winning line. But these dogs were almost too extraordinary, almost too good at what they did: now it is not
so much love as amazement with which they are regarded. The real love is accorded to the classic winners,
the dogs which battled their way through heats and
quarter finals and semifinals, which took on all-comers,
which possibly carried the dog man's ante-post bet upon
their narrow backs: the indomitable dogs, the dogs of
legs, head and heart, the dog Desert Orchids, or Red
Rums, or Mill Reefs, or Nijinskys, or Arkles, the dogs
which rose in greatness to the greatest of occasions and
took the dog men up there with them.

Mick the Miller was the first of these, and with his
staggering speed, wily brain, huge spirit and felicitous

ability to produce his best runs when it mattered most, he became the archetype of the dog man's dog. Really he set an almost impossible standard. Very few dogs have lived up to it since. Not until the 1950s did a greyhound emerge to which all dog men conceded comparable greatness; and this was Pigalle Wonder, who won the Derby in 1958.

I have a video of the history of the Greyhound Derby. It shows the race only since 1977, but it contains interviews with two or three dog men, one of whom is Arthur Hitch, trainer of the 1986 winner, Tico. He is asked which dog, his own apart, was his favourite Derby winner. As he replies, the boy in him smiles: 'I go back a few years actually' – and his voice flattens gruffly as his eyes shine with a memory which time has shaped into a mythology. 'It's got to be Pigalle Wonder. He was immaculate. And it's always stuck in my mind, seeing that big dog stroll out at the White City. It's something I shall cherish forever.'

Pigalle Wonder was one of the handsomest of all greyhounds, as arresting as a racehorse, with kindly, understanding eyes set in his sleek and lofty head. He stood high on legs that would normally be considered too long for easy running, but which he controlled to elegant and powerful effect. He was named after his owner's nightclub, the Pigalle in Piccadilly, and in the late 1950s the two Pigalles shone lights of similar brilliance into the eyes of the worldly men of post-ration book London. Al Burnett, owner of both Pigalles, was king of these men. He would stand trackside as he watched his beautiful dog, a cigar like a tiny torpedo screwed into his mouth, intimations of showgirls and champagne and largesse emanating from between the sharp, silvery folds of his silk suits.

In 1958 Pigalle Wonder won the Derby and the Pall Mall (at Harringay) and dead-heated in the Cesare-witch, which was then run over 600 yards. He also, in a race which he won by ten lengths, justifying odds of 20/1 on, set a track record for 525 yards at Wembley which remained unbeaten throughout the 17 years before metrification.

Having scraped through the first round of the 1958 Derby, edging out the fourth-placed dog by a short head – these hundredths of seconds that change lives, change mythologies! – he went on to win his semifinal by thirteen lengths, in a time (28.44) which would not be bettered for another ten years. He was, of course, odds-on favourite for the final. A tipster on the *Greyhound Express* tried to be clever and opposed him on the grounds of inconsistency: he had only won three of his last seven races. Quite so. But he was one of those dogs that won when it mattered. The opposite of Jerpoint Diamond, if you like.

The 1958 Derby final was a hard-fought, tactical affair, and in his brave and intelligent winning of it Pigalle Wonder sealed his bond of love with the dog men. He preferred the inside of the track – although not to the extent of my father's rail-hungry brood – and, having been drawn in trap 1, might have been expected to hug it all the way around. However, trap 5 got a flier and nicked the rail from him. It was not until the third bend that Pigalle Wonder, by now running second, and accepting that the gap which he sought on the rail was simply not going to appear, used his brains, nipped round on the outside and then stormed past, peeling himself away from the five dog by nearly three decisive lengths. It was an uplifting victory, because it was the victory of a dog that was not only proving its superiority, but proving that it actually wanted to win.

A greyhound, most people would say, cannot know that it is running the most important race of its life. But that isn't really so. It can certainly divine atmosphere: any dog in the world can tell the difference between a nonchalant and a galvanised crowd, let alone a dog with instincts sharp as scalpels. And some greyhounds like big occasions. They look at the crowd, they show off a little, they walk as with a purpose and they want to win. Others droop, falter, hang hot tongues downwards, blink into the lights with eyes fixed and bright with panic; and if a dog like that depends on getting out of the trap in order to win the race, then it has almost certainly lost already, because a disoriented greyhound will nearly always miss its break. As with athletes, so with dogs: when it comes to the moment of inevitable action, there are some that attack, unquestioningly and completely – Henry V greyhounds – and there are some that absent themselves, that run in a scared and obsolete dimension of their own – Hamlet greyhounds. It is the Henry V greyhounds that the dog men love. The more like Henry V the greyhounds are, the more the dog men love them.

That is why Mick the Miller and Pigalle Wonder, of all the greyhounds that have raced throughout the past sixty-six years, are the two that have attained iconical status: because they did not fear victory, they attacked it, and fought for it, and relished it. For Ballyregan Bob and Scurlogue Champ, victory was so near a certainty that they could almost disdain it; but Mick the Miller and Pigalle Wonder seemed to want it as much as the dog man feels that he himself would want it. In their quest for victory, they took the dog man, who is a fighter and a dreamer, on a journey with them. When they reached it, the dog man was up there reaching it too. These were dogs who did the dog man's striving and succeeding for him, and when they won they made him feel like a winner in his soul.

Mythologies like these have, of course, to be nurtured. In any field, consensus about what constitutes 'the greatest' grows and sustains itself like a plant, watered by both the informed and the ignorant, until nobody can remember how the roots were planted but everyone accepts that they are founded in truth. Of course there are several other greyhounds out of whose histories one could create a myth – and different dog men worship at different shrines – but just as we all have our personal gods, yet allow them to be subsumed into a communal church, so dog men may have their favourite greyhound myths, yet concede the unifying power of the Mick and Pigalle legends. They are part of the oral history of the dogs. To a dog man, the names Mick the Miller and Pigalle Wonder are like the names of Mill Reef and Nijinsky to a horse man, Muhammad Ali and Sugar Ray Robinson to a boxing man, or Pele and George Best to a footballing man – the most obvious, but still the most potent, signifiers.

Other greyhounds of lapidary name and legendary status are not myths, because they do not exert omnipotence, as a myth must do; but they have their spheres of immortality. Future Cutlet lost the 1932 Derby by a neck but won four other classics, while his brother, the great stud dog Beef Cutlet, won the 1932 Laurels in only his seventh race in England and, over a specially constructed course, ran the fastest ever 500 yards in the phenomenal time of 26.13, at a speed of over forty miles an hour (the 'real' 500 yard world record is 26.90, which was set many years later, when greyhounds were supposedly much faster, in Sydney, Australia). The white dog Model Dasher was the best to run throughout the war; there is no knowing what he might have won – the St Leger? the Cesarewitch? – had racing not been so limited at that time. Local Interprize was a magnificent trapper, a sprinter who won five classics, a record which only Mick the Miller has equalled and which nonetheless proves that a dog has to win the *right* classics if he is to become a legend. Priceless Border was beaten by only one dog throughout his racing career. He was priced at odds-on through every round of the 1948 Derby, and this confidence was justified when he won the final, disdaining its fearsomeness by leading, unchallenged, from trap to line.

Priceless Border then went to stud, where he was mated with the 1949 Derby winner, Narrogar Ann; the subsequent litter produced the 1952 Derby winner, Endless Gossip. A deliberate genetic trick had been played, by a seventy-four-year-old ex-cattle breeder who wanted a great greyhound and who applied the simplest logic to the problem of how to breed one: Derby winner plus Derby winner equals Derby winner. If only more bitches had won the Derby, the trick could have been played again to find out if it would work a second time. Certainly Endless Gossip was all that the cattle breeder could have hoped for. Effortlessly superior in every way, he was a perfect princeling, an Eton-Oxford-Palace-of-Westminster dog who almost won the Waterloo Cup, who was awarded a prize at Cruft's, who was himself a fine stud dog, and who won the Derby and the Laurels – easy, short-priced victories which signified the start of the Golden Age of greyhound racing.

Throughout the 1950s, on those post-war nights which burst with new and lovely life, the gaudy electric overspill from White City and Harringay and Wimbledon and Catford and Stamford Bridge and Wandsworth and Park Royal and New Cross and Wembley and Hendon seemed to light up London. Great greyhounds proliferated as wallets gaped and relaxed: so eager was the competition that a classic win in the 1950s was a magnificent feat, a genuine test of worth. Pigalle Wonder, emerging on to this glamorous stage like an emperor amongst kings, was proved all the greater by the simultaneous appearance of Mile Bush Pride, a dog who reached three consecutive Derby finals and won the race in 1959. Races between these two staggering brindles were possibly the finest competitions in the history of the sport. They had similar running styles in that they both liked the rails, but were intelligent enough, and competitive enough, to find any gap and go for it. This was how Pigalle Wonder won his Derby, and how Mile Bush Pride nicked his – by a neck – after a sideways shove at the first bend that would have put most dogs out of the race. He also won the Scottish and Welsh Derbies, and the Cesarewitch. Only the extreme magnetism and palpable sentience of Pigalle Wonder –

those strongly outstretched limbs, those soft and noble eyes – could possibly have overshadowed Mile Bush Pride. To have the two of them running at the same time was like having Muhammad Ali fight Jack Johnson once a month, or Carl Lewis race Jesse Owen: a superabundance in examples of supremacy, which very occasionally flows from sport like honey, but which is increasingly rare in these pinched and fiscal days: so fearful is sport of exposing the limitations of its heroes, so incapable of understanding that we relish their spirit of competition above their icy, unchallenged superiority.

In 1967, Tric Trac and his brother Spectre were winner and runner-up in the Derby. (When one thinks about how rare it is to buy a dog that *might* be good enough to run in the qualifying rounds of the race, some of the statistics attached to the Derby – winning it twice, reaching three finals, brothers coming first and second – strain credibility.) Spectre was one of the best stud dogs of the 1970s. I can remember the way in which his name recurred, like the final digit of an indivisible number, throughout the racecards of my childhood. One of his sons was Tartan Khan, that supreme economist of effort, that humorist, the dog whose greatness may be questioned but whose legendary status is not; the dog who won scarcely any race in his whole career besides the final of the Derby and the final of the St Leger.

Four years earlier, in 1971, Dolores Rocket had won the same two races. She was perhaps the best bitch ever to race, and one of only four to have ever won the Derby* – a strange statistic, since bitches are not notably slower than dogs, and no trainer or owner has ever thought to suggest that they are any less capable than dogs. There is no sexism in greyhound racing. The only real difference between male and female greyhounds is that dogs are almost always the larger; but this explains a great deal. It explains, for example, why bitches, if they are any good, tend to excel over longer distances, and why the ratio of dog-to-bitch winners for races like the Cesarewitch or the Television Trophy is far more even. Being slighter, bitches are more vulnerable; they may not be able to power their way through the rumbustious scuffles of the shorter races. The longer the race, the more chance they have to get on equal terms, even though they may get bumped over six bends or more. Amongst males also, it is usually the case that the less powerful, the less bulky the dog, the further it will run. Human athletes are exactly the same.

Dolores Rocket was a large bitch, but she was so superior anyway that she was able to pass smoothly on, leaving most scuffles to disentangle themselves behind her. (My father: 'If a dog's out of its class then it doesn't matter about bloody bumps and bends. Trouble doesn't come the dog's way.') Black and keenly beautiful, with that peculiar type of physical pride which the greatest greyhounds always seem to have – aware of themselves, yet their beauty goes far beyond what they could possibly be aware of, and so unaware of themselves as well – she was, as a game girl and a fine-looking woman, especially beloved of the dog men. More so than Westpark Mustard, the bitch who, in 1974, overtook, by one, Mick the Miller's record of nineteen consecutive wins. I was fascinated by this achievement and can remember lying awake one night when she had just broken the record, worrying over what might have gone wrong in that twentieth race – a stumble, a collision, one of those bottleneck pile-ups that happen all the time in dog racing, with Westpark Mustard at the thin and inescapable end of it. But although the feat caused a great frisson at the time, and although Westpark Mustard broke a track record and beat some of the best greyhounds racing at the time (the first of her twenty wins saw her heading off Myrtown – the greatest dog never to win the Derby), it proves that what dog men really love is a classic winner, because it is Dolores Rocket that they talk about as the greatest bitch of recent times.

Has the memory of Westpark Mustard's remarkable achievement been dimmed by the fact that she was outstripped, so overwhelmingly, by Ballyregan Bob? In photographs he stares at the camera and seems to challenge the entire future of his sport: emulate me, he seems to be saying. Try it. Win 33 races on the trot. Go faster. Look better. Can it be done? Or is Ballyregan Bob the perfect greyhound?*

Since he and Scurlogue Champ bestrode the middle 1980s like colossi, there has been no dog to touch them. The sport keeps trying to find them: Phantom Flash, who had freakish, thrilling and uncontrollable early pace; Kildare Slippy, who could jump like a stag and brought glamour back to hurdling; Druid's Johno, who was part-owned by Prince Edward, and a far more likely Derby winner than Camira Flash – except that, on 1990 final night, he was so terrorised by the noise of the crowd that he failed, for about the only time in his career, to snap out of the traps. Had he done so, his magnificent pace would have assured him legendary status. But, although a fine, fast dog, he was not a *winner*. He didn't have a winner's heart. Two years later,

Farloe Melody had such a heart. Scraping and scrambling through heats and semi-finals, through terrible trap draws and gruesome first bend pile-ups, on 1992 Derby final night he ran like a king, his strange, light, silvery brindle skin, laced as it seemed with the markings of superiority, glistening in the pools of creamy summer light. It remains to be seen how he will be remembered. Was he a fine, fast dog? Or did he have that particular quality, that apparent sentience, that thread of desire which binds him to the heart of the dog men, which will separate his name from those of the fine, fast dogs and make it sing with memories?

Our predilections for certain greyhounds can be idiosyncratic and mysterious. I always had a hankering after Indian Joe, winner of the 1980 Derby; the scenario of his story fascinated me, as did his appearance. I could almost *fancy* him when he loped out on to the stage of White City's oval arena, so sheeny, so black, so tactile was he. He made me think of polished jet, of inky silk, of sloe berries, of Joe Frazier; and to look at his coat was to feel the feel of it as if it were my own skin. I yearned to get my hands on him and stroke that shimmering nigrescence.

Sitting in his head was not the usual pair of black wounds, washed with translucent blood; instead he had a cool and casual eye, rather masculine and self-contained. He looked very much as if he knew exactly what he was doing, what his job of work was, what his instincts had fitted him for. When he allowed himself to be shovelled into the traps, he had a look on his face like that of a ravishing man who was distantly amused by his desire to seduce a not very attractive woman. After his

Derby semifinal, in which, coming from last, he had run like hell to just sneak third in a five-dog race, he seized up, crippled with cramp, and hobbled painfully off the track, stumbling and halting in a way that with most greyhounds would look unbearably pitiful, but with him looked rather fascinatingly manful. As he stuttered away, tongue low and heavy, chassis immaculate but dysfunctional, like that of a stalling Bentley, his eye rolled in his head and a crescent of white glinted out from that black satin-wrapped armature: what the fuck am I doing, it seemed to ask.

An enormous amount of money had been paid for him and, despite the cramp, the scrape into the Derby final and the fact that it was the only big race that he was ever to win, he was worth it. He was Irish, of course. I don't know how he got his name, it meant nothing, but it suited him. As a big, black baby of less than two, he had already shown his self-possession by running undaunted through the heats of the Irish Derby; his callowness only betrayed him in the final, where he finished last, no doubt rolling his eyes like mad as he walked off the track. A month later, by now fully and precociously mature, he was a close second in a big Irish open, he had become a possible contender for the English Derby and the big men were starting to take notice of him.

My father: 'I was in Ireland one year, before Indian Joe won the Derby. There was a lot of Irish talk. It said no way will this dog lose. And these blokes, they were standing at the bar talking about buying it. That was, whatsisname, Barney Eastwood, the bloke that trained Barry McGuigan. They stood in the bar, Barney and this other bookmaker, Alfie McLean, and in the end they bought the dog.'

Indian Joe had originally been bought for £500. He made his entrée into the world of the big men when he was sold to Eastwood and McLean after the first round of the Derby for a sum of not less than £25,000 and possibly as much as £35,000 (that year's prize money for winning the final). Either amount was the most that had ever been paid for a greyhound. 'Well, they made a bloody fortune, didn't they? £30,000 was a lot of money in those days, but it won the Derby. And they backed it and backed it and backed it. They knew what they were doing, didn't they? It was a risk, yes, but then, I mean, Barney's a millionaire – so is it a risk?'

Even so, what with the cramp and all, Barney and Alfie must have had cause to doubt their beautiful black dog. He had won his first round heat in a time just outside the White City track record, but then, after he changed hands, his performance plummeted, as if under the weight of all the money that was riding on his shiny back. It must have seemed to the two bookmakers that he had been spiked by a puritanical deity, one with egalitarian ideas about distribution of income, one who disapproved of men who could just nip off and buy success. Joe was second in his second round heat and third in the third, creeping into the semifinals by a couple of inches, where he again ran third. He was missing his break, he was crunched with cramp, he was bloody fed up, he was below par just when he needed to be above it; but he was still a dog amongst dogs, rolling his cool and casual eye at the opposition. 'He was something special, he was. He was entirely different class to any other dog. Oh, he was a hell of a greyhound.'

Alfie McLean, who was one of those men prepared to

pay anything to win the Derby, had had his original entry eliminated through injury, and he must have been fearful that cramp would do the same thing to Indian Joe; but the dog seemed to know that he had been designated a winner. His public seemed to know it too, because, having seen him scarcely able to walk after his semifinal, it still made him 13/8 joint favourite for the race. Word must somehow have got out that buying Joe had been Alfie and Barney's little coup; and the dog men could not presume to doubt their shrewdness, their prophetic wisdom.

Certainly the big men had bought a man of a dog. Doing what was required of him, doing the thing that he had been bought to do, he ended his story in the right, the fitting, the only way. Firmly, purposefully, nervelessly, he got on with the job and he won the Derby final. As he ran across the finishing line, he somehow looked both glorious and workmanlike.

And so the business had been done by one and all. Barney and Alfie drank deep into the night. The Irishman from whom they had bought Indian Joe lamented the loss of his dog as he toasted the £30,000 and the 33/1 ante-post price he had managed to get on him. I, sitting with my parents in White City stadium at the age of sixteen, collected the winnings from my £1 bet. And, hypnotised by the spectacle of success, we all watched Indian Joe as he stood upon the winner's rostrum: detached, handsome, nonchalant, proud, alive and sweating with the newness of victory, his coat and his trophy gleaming at each other like mirrors, and the white crescent in his black eye winking laconically, triumphantly, at the dog men, who, bursting with their ineffable emotions, surrounded him in a worshipping circle.

Indian Joe was my boy. Something about him, about the way that my father talked about him, and about the circumstances in which I saw him run (I had just finished my A levels on that 1980 Derby night, and was in a mood to fall in love with something) crystallised into a feeling which now, when I think about him, expands and glows in my head. I once met a man at the kennels who had felt that way about Commutering: 'the most popular dog to run at White City', he had sentimental-ised to me grimly, and my heart had cracked and leaked with pride. I met another man who, taking this feeling to an extreme, would simply 'adopt' another person's dog and act as if it were his own. He did this with Dolores Rocket, and got into a fight over her at West Ham sta-dium when she had been booed by some unspeakable terrace boys: she had run very badly and they had doubt-less done their money, but she had in fact gone lame, and her foster father, suffused with feelings of pity and proprietorialness, had rushed in to defend her honour. I admired him for this, although his maniacal retelling of the tale – fists aloft again, twenty years on – did hold me mesmerised by its absurdity.

Today, several dogs on, he has adopted one of our Jerpoint greyhounds. Loyalty does not prevent me from saying that this is something of a comedown from Dolores Rocket. But the loyalty of this man is absolute, and does not differentiate between the double classic winner and the Oxford grader; he runs to buy a rosette when the dog wins a race, brandishing it as if it were the Derby trophy, and his faith in the dog's ability is

implacably unrealistic in the face of my father's cur-
mudgeonly criticisms. Something in the man responds
to something in this dog, just as something in him might
respond to a person. It is this thing with dog people, that
they often react to the characteristics of greyhounds as if
they were human traits: I quickened to what I perceived
as the capable manliness of Indian Joe; our man above
fell for the streamlined beauty of Dolores Rocket and for
the buoyant, optimistic leaps of the Jerpoint dog. More
generally, dog men always talk about their bitches as if
they were women. All greyhounds are a source of frustration, but when they are female, this is even more of a
smiling matter than ever; it is as if you can't expect anything different from a woman, god bless 'em, little cows,
you've got to love 'em. When my father talks about his
bitches he is obliquely endowing them with the maddening, elusive, irresistible fascination that he thinks of as
the essence of femininity:

'Ali, she's a cow sometimes. But the reason she's
usually about is she uses her head. She looks after herself, little Ali. She won't go hurling herself into the
bends. She knew too much, she was quite clever even
when she was young.' And she hooked the son of an
earl, I expected him to continue. He is far more straight-
forward when he talks about his dogs. He makes no
concessions or excuses for them, just as he would make
none for a man; he criticises them and gives them their
due with simple judiciousness.

Conversely, dog women tend to indulge their male
greyhounds. My mother always defended the brave and
boyish Chain Gang against Pitman's Brief when my
father hinted at his preference for the bitch. Frances

Chandler told me that she fell in love with Magourna Reject when he raced into her dining room and – just like a man – wolfed a pork chop off her plate. And every week at the kennels I see a female owner who treats her big, brindle dog just as if he were her son, bustling round him, bringing him pints of milk and home-cooked food, brushing down his fur with exasperated tenderness and enjoining him to win his next race as if she were bolstering him before his school examinations; while the greyhound stands politely impassive amid all this fuss and love.

'Greyhounds are like human beings, there's good 'uns and bad 'uns. Some of them are a bloody nuisance, you know. Bite you, and do all sorts of things. Some of them are evil buggers. Some of 'em are all right.' But you like them, I asked my father – and suddenly, as if the past were the present, I saw him standing at the Hook Kennels, his head angled towards the men with whom he was talking the dog talk, as his hand fondled the sensitive brindle ears of his boy, his great-hearted winner, his beloved Commutering. 'Ah yes. I like them. The only trouble is you like some of them better than others, don't you? It's natural. It's only the same as liking people.'

8

Out of Ireland

Like most dog people, we have always bought our grey-hounds in Ireland. In the early 1970s, my father found a breeder from whom he was to get all his dogs for the next ten years or so, but before that he came by them rather more haphazardly.

'Oh, I remember once, when I bought a dog – it would have been in the late sixties – I was with Tommy (a Greek dog man). We were driving along some road, I don't know where we were, and there was a little old boy with a fawn and a red dog. Stop the car, Tom said. "Do you want to sell them, boy?" He got on well with the Irish, Tom did. And the old boy said, "Yes." And one of these dogs, well, he won the Midland Puppy Derby. £100 I paid for him. And Tom paid £300 for his brother. Which was useless.

'And we went back to the house with this little old boy – and his old mum, oh, she was very worn out, you could see that – and it was just a little shed, a little stone build-ing about half the size of this room. I shall always remember it, because we bought these dogs, and she got this bottle of whisky and poured it out into three glasses – Christ. There was a Madonna there, standing on a shelf, and I hid mine behind that. I don't know what Tom did with his.

'They hadn't even got a toilet. The men had to go and wee behind a wall. It was real poverty. And we slung these dogs in the back of the car and that was that. We didn't know if they were any good. We looked at the books, and the dogs had had trials, and that was how we used to do it. We might have taken them up the schooling track, I can't remember. It's a long time ago.

'But everyone knew Tom the Greek. I tell you, we went to Thomastown, near Kilkenny, one year, and the word went round that Tom the Greek was there. They used to send the message out. On Sunday morning in the square they used to turn up in their bloody droves with these dogs. They'd bring 'em up on their leads for Tom to inspect, and he'd buy 'em, if he liked the look of anything. "How much do you want for it?" And it'd be twice as much as they eventually got. There'd probably be a hundred or more dogs in that square on a Sunday morning. And they'd all be world beaters. All the men'd have a tale to tell.

'I remember Tom turning up at the airport, he had a white carrier bag with him. I said what you got there Tom? He said, I've got my clothes. But I tell you what, he knew everyone in southern Ireland. And everyone knew him. Tom the Greek's in town – it used to go round like on the bloody drums. They've got some way of communicating with each other over there. None of them have got telephones. But they know, don't they? And they're all twisters, the dog men. They play the same record every time you try and do a deal with them, and they know they're not going to get it. At the schooling track in Thomastown, we'd take the dogs round –

well, the bloke that used to time them, he was in league with the breeders. We never used to trust him. Used to time them ourselves, under our sleeves.

'Jerry H was with us there once. That was where he tried to buy that dog that was about nine foot tall. We went in this pub, and butcher's shop, you know, one of each, we had a drink and Tom said, "You got any dogs?" "Oh, I've got dogs out the back," he said. "Got a fine dog." So he brings this dog in, and I've never seen such a tall dog. Bloody great thing with legs you could drive a bus under. And, I tell you what, we really had to fight Jerry H to stop him from buying it. He was drinking gin like it was going out of fashion, and he was determined to buy this bloody dog. We managed to stop him. But I've never seen a dog as tall as that. They'd never have got it in a trap.

'But Tommy got Jerry his own really good dog. And I know where he bought it, 'cos I've been there with him. It was where they sat on stones in the living room, and the beds – you climbed up a ladder and got in the loft. They had a hole in the ceiling. That – well, that was something else, that was. That was an education. You've never seen such a bloody place. They were really, really peasants. Up to your knees in mud, more holes in this bloody barn than not, dogs everywhere coming in and out, what a bloody place it was. But this man bred some good greyhounds. That dog of Jerry's, its sire was one of the best stud dogs ever. And the man would have had his own brood bitch.

'But breeders those days didn't make any money. That was Ireland in the sixties, seventies. They wouldn't be sitting on stones now. But in those days there were no cars around, nothing. I think breeders make a bit more nowadays – but still there's loads of people like that in Ireland. It's a bloody hard life breeding dogs. But it's part of their life in Ireland, there aren't many places where there isn't somebody breeding dogs. And then you get the odd shrewd one. Jack Mullan, he was a legend in the game. He was the biggest man in dog racing. He was a breeder and trainer in Ireland, and he used to win the Derby, track and course, regularly. He died two or three years ago. I remember going to his place with Jerry H, and when we got there you couldn't get near his kennels. He had about twelve stud dogs there, and the bloody vehicles outside with the bitches coming to be served – they were queuing up! But he had all the crack stud dogs. Big man. They used to name races after him. He was a rich man 'n' all.

'We went over the border to get to his place; he was in Newry. That was the only time I went to the north. I didn't particularly like it. We stayed in this hotel, and there was an atmosphere – we were in IRA country, I think. Mind you, we went over to Clonmel one year, and we took this old boy with us who'd never been to Ireland before – Christ, what a pain he was. What a bloody coward. He wouldn't go in an Irish pub. These pokey little holes that were pubs, he could see bloody IRA behind every curtain. Frightened him to death.'

My father would go to Ireland two or three times a year, for the coursing at Clonmel and to buy grey-hounds. He, and men like him, are well-known figures in the Irish dog world – he could probably still introduce himself as the man that owned Commutering – a world which crosses over with the other worlds of life far more closely, extensively and naturally than it does over here. The Irish are bred to breed racing animals. By that I don't mean, of course, that they all do so; but those that do have an instinct for it, while those that don't have an instinctive understanding of that instinct. The Irishman's relationship with the racing animal is symbiotic, easy, unquestioning. So ancient and indestructible is the bond between the Irishman and his greyhound that he can worship it for what it represents and, at the same time, without any thought of contradiction, treat it with the simple, businesslike cruelty of the livestock farmer. For all his charm, for all his talk, the Irishman's heart is cold towards his greyhound. It never seems to leak with sentiment in the way that the English dog man's constantly threatens to do. Sentiment is in the Irish dog man's tongue, not in his heart.

Perhaps that is why, on the whole, the Irish breed better greyhounds. The necessary attitude, one of absolute understanding and absolute ruthlessness, comes naturally to them: they think nothing of it. British breeders can acquire this attitude, but to the Irishman it is unconsidered. It is part of his instinctive ruralism; and it is also, I think, connected with the way in which he has been shaped by his country's tragic history. This history, which the Irishman carries around with him like a calling card, has bred in him a fatalism, a feeling for the way in which events repeat themselves and are never resolved; and it has also bred in him a desire constantly to strike out from this unbreakable cycle. Somehow, this contradictory, questing fatalism has fitted him for life with the racing animal. He is resigned to the cyclical nature of this life, but he is besotted, he is in love with its occasional tangents: the gambling wins, the successful coups, the champion dogs.

My father: 'They're all seeking, the Irish. They're the same with horses as well. They'll breed with last year's Derby winner and then, next year, instead of breeding with that again, they'll breed with the current winner – looking for something better. They're not satisfied. Our breeder likes to use unknown stud dogs. He used Manorville Sand and we got Jerpoint Diamond, but now he's top line he doesn't want to use him. I mean, chances are we'd have got another Diamond if we'd gone back to Manorville Sand, but he wants something better.'

And, of course, the Irishman's history has rendered him finally indifferent, beneath the haunting tune that his fabled charm reprises to the world. 'Too long a sacrifice can make a stone of the heart': the Irishman wears his tattered nationalism like motley partly because it is expected of him, and partly because, after so long, there is little else he can do. And so he smiles, and he shrugs, and he sings, and he tells his tales, and he seems to find it easy to be cool, or even cruel, thus to preserve his besieged self, within its shell of cooing haplessness.

One needs to be cool, or even cruel, in the business of breeding greyhounds. For it *is* a business, and even those breeders who make no money at it still treat it as such. These dogs are commodities. There are certain elements that these commodities must possess before they can even be considered as saleable. If a greyhound is physically inadequate, or won't chase the electric hare, or won't run round a track, or fights, or is simply too slow, then it is useless, a reject, eliminated at the first quality check, and the only thing to do with it is to destroy it. I was told a story of an Irish breeder who took two pups for their first run around a schooling track. When, at this very first attempt, they failed to chase the hare, he stopped at the vet on the way home and had them put down. Those puppies crawling blindly round their mother's sleek and valuable limbs have entered a rigorous world of hard, hard men.

But pets, as my father always tells me, don't make racing dogs. And the wildness in greyhounds has to be preserved. That atavistic instinct is the fire at the heart of dog racing. If that is extinguished, then everything goes: the lights around the stadia, the contest between the bookmakers and the gamblers, the night out, the sport, the dog men, the dogs – they all would be gone, if the greyhound lost its desire to chase the hare. And so the Irish breeder rears his greyhounds hard. He sharpens their ferity until their muzzles are keen as stilettoes and their ears twitch like antennae. He keeps them tough, he keeps them wild at heart, and he keeps his sport alive.

My father: 'In Ireland they let them rough it at an early stage, in a barn. They run amok until they're about fourteen months. They've got to else you've got a litter of pets. I knew a man in Cappoquin, in Waterford, he was up the side of a mountain and he'd never got half his dogs. He used to come into town for a car tyre, set light to it and put an oil drum on it, then he'd boil their grub up in it – slop a lot of old vegetables and meat in it, then shovel it up and feed 'em. Mrs G at White City had a champion from him. But half his dogs he couldn't get: he never caught 'em.

'They do have a big percentage of losses – weeds that can't fend for themselves, or some that just go, or get killed. Well, they do, running wild. It's nobody's fault. Every dog of mine that comes over from Ireland has got slits in it where it's had lumps taken out and then been sewn up.

'The English don't rear 'em that way. They've learned a lot, but they don't let them keep running around for days. They keep 'em in little paddocks, and they get bored, they get fat, they start fighting. You've got these beautiful looking dogs in English paddocks, well bred and all that but, some of them, they either fight or they don't chase. Now, I've never owned a dog that hasn't chased.'

At about fourteen months, the wild greyhounds are tamed, at least externally: taught to walk on a lead, kennelled, disciplined for the work ahead of them. Opinions differ on whether or not they need to be trained for their job, or whether it comes so naturally to them that this is unnecessary.

My father: 'They *used* to have to be schooled to run round a track, but it's a fallacy now when they say, "Oh, you've got to school 'em before you send them over." School the buggers?! You give them a few handslips, put them in the traps and they're away. They don't need the schooling they used to need because, as they've kept interbreeding with track dogs, they've become track dogs. They don't learn to track only by going on the track. You can't teach 'em. Some silly buggers say, "Oh, he wants a few lessons out of the traps." But a dog learns. They go in the traps and when they get left behind all the time they think, well, I must stand still, or I must do something, and get out a bit sharpish.

'But some of the English-bred ones, they just don't

come out of the boxes. And it's cruel, because they're no good. They've got to be reared running wild. When they're domesticated there's not a better dog in the world. But deep down they're savage. They've got to be.'

I can remember one day, taking out Ali and Daley from the kennels. I had dawdled the few hundred yards that I adjudged a walk (greyhounds are lazy, too, oddly enough) with two quiescent angels dangling from my wrist. They had ambled ahead of me as I dreamily swooned over their tightened waists and wobbling ribs; jiggled biscuits in my pocket as I waited to get the dogs home and win their ravenous love; showed off to passing cars as I swanned along with my beautiful charges, like a mother with a newly-filled Harrods pram. All was Sundayish, relaxed, idyllic in its small, intense way.

Then a small terrier erupted into the distant view. The pull on my arms frightened me with its suddenness. Inside the muzzles, the jaws of my dogs slackened and slavered to let out whines of a desire so strong that it sounded like pain; I thought of men in jail, clutching ferociously at bars as a naked woman weaved past them. The sleek bodies were bunched and prancing, limbs splayed like Dickensian starvelings, tails stiff and swishing like dangerous reptiles. It was as if they were straining to exact revenge upon the object which had aroused this unbearable passion in them. It must be what they look like in the traps. There too, they are being gripped, over and over and over again, by the need to sate that love in them for the pointless chase and the purposeless kill.

It's what they have to be like. And there *is* one English breeder who turns them out this way, with all their primal instincts sharp as switchblades; he may not be the only one, but he is certainly the best. In 1992, I saw three of his greyhounds win the Grand Prix, the Gold Collar and – of course – the British Breeders' Stakes; I saw five of them run in one St Leger. Nicky Savva has been producing dogs of superb quality for years and years. My father: 'The master breeder. No argument about that, he's a master at his trade.

'All breeders think it's the bitches that do it. If you haven't got a good brood bitch then you've got nothing. Savva's got his bitches' blood lines right. He still gets bad dogs, yes, but only a very small percentage. He had a litter from one stud dog recently and they weren't much. Well, the dog can't be any good at stud, because he gave him one of his best bitches and the dogs are quite mediocre. Now the next litter she had, she had from Daley's Gold and they're ruling the world.'

As if to signify that he is the equal of the Irish breeder with his prefixes, his signature tunes, his Monalees and Manorvilles, Nicky Savva has his own English prefix – his dogs are named after his Westmead Kennels in Bedfordshire – and I can recall a score of these Westmead greyhounds running in big race finals, standing tall at stud and mothering more magnificent Westmeads. Westmead County, Westmead Power, Westmead Champ, Westmead Move, Westmead Suprise and Westmead Spirit (these last two sisters, daughters of Westmead Move, ran first and second in the 1992 Gold Collar); it is an unbroken chain which, over the last twenty years or so, has become a dog dynasty as integral to the sport as the Chandler family. It is a stream as unstoppable as a waterfall, and there seems to be no reason why it should ever dry up, because the Westmead breeding has become so refined and superabundant: there is unlikely now ever to be a dearth of brood bitches with immaculate blood and childbearing hips. The challenge now is to find for these intricately, richly, purely bred women some decent men. They are the daughters of an aristocratic house, and as such they must be suitably mated.

The difficulties burgeon – as with the aristocracy – because there is no way of knowing what will make a good stud dog. All the classic winners, the speed merchants, the beaten finalists, they will all go off and lead their lives of limitless sex, like dog Don Giovannis, yet when one comes to study the racecards one will see the same names coming up over and over again. Today it would be Daley's Gold, Manorville Sand, Flashy Sir, with Druid's Lodge coming up fast on the outside. In my childhood it was Maryville Hi, The Grand Silver, Moordyke Spot and a couple of others; but most dominant of all were Spectre and Monalee Champion.

Spectre was born to one of the best litters ever – only Westmead Move has thrown one as good: one brother won the Derby and another the St Leger. The probability of scoring such a clutch of dogs in one hit is so remote as to be incalculable. This shouldn't be so, because if one dog in a litter is decent then the tightly controlled laws of greyhound breeding should decree that all the others be decent also; but what actually happens is that all the blood gets concentrated in one – or sometimes two – dogs. And anyway, even if one were to get a whole litter of fine runners, the likelihood of getting a litter of *winners*, of dogs with winning hearts, is something else altogether.

But what is really extraordinary about Spectre is that

the litter from which he came was so good that one would think it must surely be the end of a line; an apex from which there must be a falling off. The blood in it was so rich that it must, surely, taint and curdle thereafter. It is as if two well-bred people – he an aristocrat, say, she of the vestigially peasant stock that would put robustness into his etiolated lines and a chin on to the end of his face – were to produce a series of dream children; scholars, athletes, beauties; kindly, zestful, equable. What might these paragons then go on to produce? Renegade Etonians, drug addicts, suicidal mannequins, inexplicable runts. The cycles of nature demand that perfection cannot last, that it cannot be inherited. The world, and all the other people in it, wouldn't stand for it.

Yet Spectre's blood was somehow still new inside him, and he threw great dogs at stud. This is extraordinary; even in dog genetics it is unusual. The very best racers seldom make the very best sires, although people will always hurl their brood bitches at them the instant that they step off the track and on to their gigolo beds; one can only assume that they disappoint as sires because they represent the predestined end of that particular strain of breeding. Mick the Miller was nothing special at stud. Scurlogue Champ was impotent. Ballyregan Bob has thrown one or two excellent dogs, but when one imagines the number of bitches he must have got through then the percentage of winners is small. If I were looking for a sire then I would never go to a dog like him – so obvious, so perfect, so liable to disappoint. I would look for a greyhound like Monalee Champion, who was not so much a winner of races as an embodier of certain qualities that bespoke untapped depths, hope, potential. My father: 'He wasn't a great dog. He was a good dog. He didn't win a lot but he had this tremendous middle pace, this acceleration, which you used to see up the back straight.' Spectre was a better dog, in that he won more races, but I suspect that what made him such a good stud dog was not so much the winning of races as the variety of distances over which these races were won. He was second in the Derby over 525 yards; won the Midland St Leger over 700 yards; and won the TV Trophy over 880 yards. This combination of early, middle and finishing pace is extremely rare. It meant that Spectre had a body full of riches that he could will to his children; three possible qualities with which a bitch might coalesce.

Of course the breeding of Spectre and Monalee Champion was, in itself, superb. The blood of supreme stud dogs was racing through their veins, its influence still vibrating and viable; dogs who made greyhounds what they are today; dogs of an importance that could only be possible when the sport was young and developing. Both Spectre and Monalee had the same sire, Crazy Parachute. He was a son of Hi There, who was the finest sire of the 1950s and 1960s. They also both contained the blood of Mad Tanist, a dog who, like Phantom Flash half a century later, was so fast out of the traps that he couldn't control his speed and would slide into the first bend almost horizontal. Mad Tanist's early pace was even more freakish than Phantom Flash's, or perhaps he was simply less able to handle it; but he passed the seed of it on to his children, thus breeding a whole new superior race of what my father calls 'out-

and-gone merchants', those oh-so precious dogs which shoot from traps like cannonballs, lead to the first bend and stream clear and free of the snarling knot behind them.

In the late 1940s, the Mad Tanist progeny was inter-bred with that of Castledown Lad, who was a dog of unusual stamina and finishing power. When these two blood lines were locked together, complimenting and completing each other as they did, the breeding lines of greyhounds were transformed, for at the junction of these two lines there lay, in fact, the possibility of perfection. By this union, greyhounds were made into finished articles. Now at last they were really track dogs, *racers*, coursing crossovers no longer. Indeed the conjoining of these two dog houses was a dynastic marriage that any sixteenth century ruler would have been proud of. Pigalle Wonder was an early scion.

The blood of Mad Tanist, of Castledown Lad, of Hi There, and, now, of Monalee Champion and Spectre can be traced in the pedigree of any greyhound racing at any licensed track in Britain today. Which is why, when one talks about breeding, as in 'he's a superbly bred dog', or 'his blood lines are right', I am always tempted to think how absurd – they are *all* well bred. Sixty-six years is too short a time for there to have accrued whole families full of bad blood. All you get are the one-off misfits, which are so ruthlessly pulled from the breeding soil. In a way, there is no reason why any racing dog at all might not throw a champion – after all, plenty of champions throw scrubbers – since there would be nothing wrong with his breeding. Of course that would never be tried. It would be too much of a risk, as if breeding greyhounds isn't enough of a risk anyway.

There is no doubt that the breeding of greyhounds improved in the 1950s. Nor is there any doubt that this improvement was there to be made: the dogs were metamorphosing from coursers to trackers. They and their sport had a big leap forward to make. But now there is no improvement to be made, not really. If the dogs get any faster they will kill themselves running into those vicious bends; if they get any stronger they will be unable to negotiate either each other or the tracks. They are, today, like 100-metre athletes: at the limit of what God has given them. Perhaps for the rest of time they will have only hundredths of seconds left to play with.

Which means that all a greyhound breeder can do today is maintain the standard. To be able to do this he needs, in my opinion, three unquantifiable talents. The first is timing, an ability to sense when the blood in a greyhound is new, to sort the Monalee Champions from the Ballyregan Bobs; the second is a matchmaking instinct, a sense of which dog house would marry well with which, a vision of which male and female would bring out the best in each other; and the third is the talent that any dog man needs who yearns to make a success of his sport: that of knowing his greyhounds. He has to penetrate as far as he can the mystery of what is inside their head and heart. He has to be intimate with every nuance of their bodies, every idiosyncrasy of their running, every variation of their temperaments. Because the whole business is concerning itself with fractions of seconds. As with 100-metre athletes, it is the niceties of predetermined physical conformation, together with the enigmas of desire, and desire to achieve desire, which will separate the contenders from the also-rans and the champions from the contenders.

But if a dog breeder needs these unquantifiable talents, then, like the creatures that he breeds, what he needs at least as much is luck. Yes, judgement is necessary; yes, a man like Nicky Savva seems, through painstaking refinement, to have eliminated luck from the equation. But what seems to me to prove that luck is still the most important factor is that, in the history of greyhound racing, there have been so few litters like Spectre's, litters which contain more than two dogs of fine and parallel ability. Why, if the breeding of greyhounds can be controlled, do the good dogs only come singly or in pairs? Why only them in the litter? What ordained that Ballyregan Bob should have been the most perfect greyhound of all time? Why should he not have been like his brothers and sisters? Why should his brothers and sisters not have been like Bob? What breeding system can account for Scurlogue Champ? What magical mysteries coalesced in him to conjure those unearthly powers?

The truth is that just as the gambling man cannot entertain the thought that, ultimately, luck is the prime factor ordaining his success or failure, just as he must allow himself his systems and his form cards and his belief that he controls the future, so the breeding dog man must allow himself his theories and his stud books and his belief that he controls the future. He cannot allow himself fully to entertain a thought such as this one: that the reason why some of these good stud dogs *are* good stud dogs is because they get so many bitches that the law of probability decrees that they will throw some decent pups. But then only the most cynical, or well-adjusted, among us would be able to acknowledge the true importance of luck in our lives.

*

When I stood that day with my father at the kennels, watching the pups that had come over from Ireland, I was in the wonderful dream world of absolute anticipation and could see no reason why these dogs should be anything but champions. As soon as they started trialling, I could see no reason why they should even be able to run properly. I had been struck, for the first time in my dog days, by just how much one takes for granted about these greyhounds: the standards that are set for them, the number of things that one expects them to be able to do. Yes, they have been bred to run round a track, but I have been bred to understand simple mathematics and I can't do it. Yes, their instinct is to chase a hare, but my instinct should have got me married off by now and it hasn't. Yes, they are meant to be able to run 450 metres in less than twenty-nine seconds, but I am meant to be able to function on eight hours' sleep a night and I need nine and a half. This isn't really a fair parallel: I am not a thoroughbred scion of a purpose-built species; I do not have what is effectively a sixty-six-year ancestry. The variations possible within racing greyhounds are limited, because their history is limited. But even so, thinking about those pups, just about to start doing the job for which they had been bred and indeed born – and thinking, of course, about the one amongst them that might be unable to do this job – I realised how little one remarks the fact that is *is* hundredths of seconds which separate so many of them; that so many of them *are* able to do the thing that they are meant to do; that breeding really *does* work to such an extent.

But to the dog men – breeders, owners, trainers – this fact is not enough. They have got far more important things to worry about than the expense of wonder on the consistency of thoroughbreeding: that, they think, is the least they can hope for. A lifetime spent following a clutch of adequate, graded greyhounds is what many dog men will have, but it is not what they want. Always, always, always they will be looking for the dog that shears off those hundredths of seconds, the dog of perfectly planned yet mysterious provenance, the dog whose name, in years to come, will sing with memories. And then, even if they get such a dog, they will be looking for another, and a better. They might be plain, worldly, down-to-earth people, but they are brindled with hope.

After the trawling days round Thomastown with Tommy A, the days of sitting on stones and hiding whisky behind Madonnas, my father found a breeder and stayed with him for about ten years. This may be less fun, but it is the best way of supplying oneself with greyhounds. If one had been in with Jack Mullan, for example, one might almost automatically have become a dog man to be reckoned with; the thing, of course, would have been to have had the acumen, the *timing*, to have got in with him before he became the biggest man in greyhound racing.

Michael B, who lived in Co. Waterford, had bred Commutering. He sold him to an Englishman who took him to Frank Melville, then a trainer at Hook Kennels, from whom he was sold to my father – for £250, incidentally, which was a bargain even in 1971. (So keen was Frank to get my father to buy this dog – he sensed that my father would make a decent owner, and that the dog would make a decent greyhound – that he rang him with an inventory of reasons, the last of which was, desperately, 'And, do you know, his kennel name's Andrew!'). This is my father's name. It wasn't Commutering's, and my mother never went along with it. 'He was always Jackie to me,' she would say, if she wanted an oblique snub to her husband; but at the kennels, where they wanted an oblique compliment, the dog became Andy. (All dogs have kennel names. Some are rather nice – London Lights was known as Paddy – but often they are of an unwieldy, plonking, human variety, ill-suited to these fine-boned exquisites. After the Show was Bill. The beautiful Chain Gang was Cyril.)

Anyway, the felicitous introduction of Andy to Andy led Andy the man to Andy the dog's breeder. Michael's bungalow teemed with children, his grounds teemed with greyhounds, and the air around them teemed with the naturalness of fecundity: the commonplace miracle. I was in heaven when I visited the place in my earliest adolescence, spending long warm hours with my face buried in the necks of greyhounds and, incongruously, in the short and wiry coat of a small Jack Russell – as if they didn't have enough dogs there – but that dog, I realise now, was a pet. The others were commodities.

Although the first dog that Michael supplied, albeit indirectly, to my father was in fact the best – thus setting a standard to which hope would rise, in true dog-man fashion, with every new-born greyhound – he did continue to breed for him an unusually high proportion of open racers. After the Show, whom my father snapped up with beady immediacy, won the Wood Lane Stakes at White City. Chain Gang won the Regency. Pitman's Brief's track record at Catford needed Scurlogue

Champ to break it (although he did scissor nearly a second off it, the bugger). Fit Me In won the Essex Vase at Romford. Killoneford Dash won the Long Hop Chase, the hurdle race run at White City on Derby nights. Sun Chariot won the Midland Flat at Hall Green (at a price, I seem to remember, of 25/1). All these races are not-quite classics. They are the aristocracy, but not the monarchy, of the greyhound racing hierarchy – just as, I suppose, these dogs are the aristocracy, but not the monarchy, of greyhound racing history – although love and loyalty make me say that it was bad luck, rather than deficiency, which decreed that Commutering and Chain Gang did not win the St Leger, that Chain Gang or Pitman's Brief did not win the Cesarewitch. Yes, their tracking let them down, but, in dog racing, tracking works in partnership with luck as well as speed. If a fast dog wants the rails and a gap appears there, then that fast dog will probably win the race. The gaps didn't appear often enough for these greyhounds. In dog racing, one should always remember that unless the greyhound is a supreme phenomenon that dances upon luck as if walking on water, superior to the extent that its owner can exude serenity rather than that hysterical fatalism which owners usually do exude, smother it though they will in smiles – unless the greyhound is a great greyhound, then winning a race will imply many things about a dog, but above all it will imply that it had more than one-sixth of the luck. My father's dogs always seemed to get about a tenth.

I think of Michael with much affection because he gave me London Lights. The partnership dissolved between him and my father, as these close alliances will, but he is now one of the top breeders in Ireland, having earned the luck – for sometimes both dogs and dog men earn it – to provide Prince Edward with Druid's Johno, the dog that should have won the 1990 Derby. My father's breeder is now Pat F, of Kilkenny and the Jerpoint prefix.

A good breeder may be the safest place to get one's greyhounds, but the owner still has to know his dogs in order to make a success of it. He might have to pick two or three sixteen-month-old pups out of a litter, which, as my father says, 'is very difficult. An ordinary person can't pick between a common one and a classy one. You'd only pick a baby on a whim and a fancy, but at sixteen months, given a couple of hours, you could . . .'

Why do you need a couple of hours, I asked.

'Well, they don't stand still, do they?'

I asked my father if he would be able to say what he was looking for in them. 'Not really, no. If I see one . . . Of course, you can get it wrong. I mean, I can remember that dog that held a couple of track records – can't think of its name. Well, I wouldn't have given it house room, terrible common looking dog; but that was a little bit freakish. Well, you go and see six Derby finalists, see if there's any rags amongst them.'

That is true, of course. One might think that all greyhounds look much the same. Then one sees a greyhound of true class, and one's perceptions are excited by the leap that they have to make in order to appreciate what they are perceiving. Just to look at a photograph of Ballyregan Bob makes my throat constrict with admiration and my chin jerk up with empathetic physical arrogance; I am always reminded of an early evening driving through Earls Court, when alongside my crawling car flowed streams of dogs emerging from Cruft's. Everything about them seemed exaggerated to the extremest edges of acceptability. Some of them had necks that looked as if they had been stretched in a noose; some of them were as tall as dinner tables; some of them courted emaciation; and they all walked like ballerinas through minefields. I couldn't believe that they were out there in the road, indenting the real world with their magical-dimensional progress. This is a feeling that I get when I look at certain greyhounds. If something looks like that, I feel, then it ought to have another world to inhabit.

Class can be perceived not so much by what one is looking at, as by the effect that looking at it has upon one. When I look at nice, cheap clothes, I may feel pleasure; but when I go into Brown's and look at designer stuff then I feel tense, I feel restless, I feel a kind of yearning, a space forms inside of me that will never now be filled by anything less than this shimmering perfection. Of course this feeling comes partly because I already *know* that what I am looking at is superior – how can it not? But, when one beholds class, anticipation of how fine it will be rushes to meet perception of how fine it indeed is; the two collide, and inside one something breaks, releasing a faintly bitter balm. That is how I feel when I look at Ballyregan Bob. He is so classy, so perfect, that I cannot quite deal with it. I suppose this is because his appearance: contained, other, entirely defined – constitutes a judgement upon my own: assailed, known, stragglingly human.

As my father says, when one sees the six Derby finalists parading round the track, then one will feel the presence of class. But that is easily felt. It might even have been easy when the greyhounds were sixteen months old. Nor would one have to be a dog person to feel it. But it is not so easy to *grade* dogs, to distinguish the ordinary greyhound from the minor open racer, the A6 dog from the A1, to locate the tiny faults in conformation that might slow down a dog by fractions of seconds. To me there are the classy looking ones, the decent looking ones, and the ordinary looking ones; but to be honest, I should be hard put to tell between a decent looker and an ordinary looker unless I had the two of them side by side. It gets easier, but judging a dog in isolation takes either the experience or the instinct of the dog man. I was at the kennels recently, talking to my father's trainer about dog appearances, when he pointed out to me a greyhound that was running round a pen. 'Look at him!' he said. 'Yes!' I coasted. 'He's one of the fastest dogs at Oxford.' 'Is he?' I said, my eyes worrying away at him as I tried to see something remarkable. 'You can't believe it, can you?' 'No!' I said, tutting with relief, 'you can't!' 'He's a real weed, look at him.' By which time I could see that he was a weed – although, in this instance, it would have been a good thing that I couldn't see it, because the dog was indeed one of the fastest dogs at Oxford.

'He is. He's a smashing little dog,' said my father. 'But he's a freak. You do get these freak dogs. But the thing is, you've got to go on something, haven't you? Conformation and behaviour, that's what I go on. They've got to be properly made-up and they've got to be properly behaved. Good dogs are usually good dogs. If they're a bloody nuisance they're usually bloody useless.'

The theory of the calm, mannerly champion is one of the many accepted wisdoms in the sport, and it is, like most of them, true in the main. Again, however, there are freaks. Wild Woolley, who won the Derby in 1932, loved biting people, especially his vet; and Balliniska Band, who won the race in 1977, was, on his own trainer's admission, a 'headcase' whose idea of fun was to gnaw his way through his kennel door. However, contrary to the ideas that many people seem to have about them, and despite the fact that they have been bred as fine as an electric wire, greyhounds are rarely neurotic or vicious. I have known shy ones, and offhand ones, and lunatic ones, but never unlovable ones. They are almost always sweet natured and all too desirous of the occasional, unexpected touch of human affection.

Freaks aside, tranquillity, size and strength in a greyhound are what a dog man wants. A good sprinting dog will tend to be 'short-coupled' – to have a compact back, with front and hind legs close together – and it will be very powerful across the chest and shoulders, and around the thighs and haunches. A staying dog will probably have a longer back, and a rangier step that prevents it snapping out of the traps. It won't necessarily weigh less, but it may look finer, more extended around the limbs.

The best male greyhounds usually weigh between 70 and 77 pounds; the best bitches between 60 and 70 pounds. Good dogs, both male and female, will almost always have very deep chests, as well as long, firm necks, big backsides and thick thighs. Otherwise they will be 'weeds' which, unless they are also 'freaks', will lack power and pace.

What I look for in the conformation of a greyhound, and the thing that gives me most pleasure to see, is that springy, imminent-looking curvature that correlates the dipping chest with the swelling haunches. It forms a strongly-coiled S shape, with the waist at its evanescent centre, which bunches and extends itself as the dog moves. I am looking at the greyhound as if it were a living sculpture, because to me it is simply the most beautiful animal on earth. I do not think to look for the physical defects which might slow it up by a tenth of a second, because I am not a true dog person. My father, however, like any dog man, silently worships the greyhound, but even as he is admiring its extraordinary aesthetic he is checking it over to make sure he is not doing his money.

'You've got to look at their necks; you've got to see they've got a good back end on them; you've got to make sure they're straight of hock. They don't run right unless their hocks are right. Like that pup, the one that runs off the track – he's got a dodgy hock. I told you that the first day I saw him, didn't I? Ali's got good straight hocks, but she's a *little* bit short in the leg' (there is an obverse fault, where a dog will be said to have 'too much daylight under it', like the one in the pub at Thomastown) 'and a little bit thick in the back. She's quite – she's a bit above average, but she's not a *quality* looking dog.

'Of course, if Mick the Miller was around today he'd be a common dog.' Yes, he would; there is nothing in the conformation of his stuffed outline at the Natural History Museum to suggest that he could collect tracks between his feet with such ease and speed. Greyhounds have physically changed in the sixty-six years of the dogs. Yet one can read a fourteenth-century treatise on hunting by Edmund de Langley, son of Edward III and Master of Hounds to Henry IV, in which he describes his ideas of what constitutes perfection in a greyhound, and recognise the dog one walked last Sunday at the kennels:

[it] should have a long hede and somedele grete, yma-kyd in the manner of a luce; a good large mouth and good sessours, the one again the other, so that the nether jaws passe not them above, ne that thei above passe not him by neither.

The neck should be grete and longe, and bowed as a swanne's neck.

Her shuldres as a roebuck; the for leggs streght and grete ynow, and nought to hind legges; the feet straught and round as a catte, and great cleas; the boones and the joyntes of the cheyne [backbone] grete and hard as the chyne of an hert; the thighs great and squarred as an hare; the houghs streight, and not crompyng as of an oxe.

A catte's tayle, making a ring at eend, but not to hie.

Of all maners of Greihounds there byn both good and evel; Natheless the best hewe is rede falow, with a black moselle.

I can't agree with this last statement: dark fawn dogs with black faces are the enormous coursing greyhounds of my nightmares – and probably of Edmund de Langley's sweetest dreams. To me, and I think perhaps to a lot of dog people, the best-looking greyhounds are either black or brindle. There is something about those coats – redolent as they are of the panther and the tiger – that makes a greyhound look perfectly dressed for its job, just as the sheen of lycra upon black skin befits an athlete more than white cotton flapping round ecru thighs. The fact that Mick the Miller, Beef Cutlet, Future Cutlet, Endless Gossip, Pigalle Wonder, Mile Bush Pride, Tartan Khan, Ballyregan Bob, Farloe Melody, Commutering and After the Show were all brindles; and that Local Interprize, Spectre, Dolores Rocket, Indian Joe, Tico, Scurlogue Champ, Chain Gang and Pitman's Brief were all black, is merest coincidence – although it too goes to explain the innate trust that I invest in dogs of these colours. They are class until proved scrubbers.

But it is only when Edmund de Langley writes on colour that I am in disagreement with him. Everything else could have been written today, except that today it would be expressed far more dully and effetely. These similes are a joy; they are so substantial and savoury one can almost taste them; and so directly apt, so unconsciously poetical, using, as they do, other animals for illustration. I should never have thought of likening a greyhound's thighs to those of a hare, its neck to a swan's, its feet to a cat's, but the description gives one the look of the dog clearly and immediately. My father's similes, which derive from the urban and human world, rather than the natural world of animals, have their own evocativeness. I know what he means when he says that a greyhound has a robust chest like John Regis's, or rangy legs like Linford Christie's, or barrow-boy feet like Jimmy White's, or no neck like Gladstone Small; but what is most interesting about the points that he is thus making is that they are exactly the same as Edmund de Langley's. The racing greyhound may, in its brief life, have metamorphosed from a courser to a tracker; it may have acquired a finesse, a definition, an evermore precise and purposeful beauty, composed of power and delicacy in equal parts; but in its essentials, it has an ancient constancy.

The Dogs

There is a letter in a twenty-year-old edition of the *Greyhound Magazine* which asks, so politely and humbly that it reads almost as a plea, that the sport of greyhound racing consider the setting up of homes for its unwanted dogs. Not just for the ex-racers, but for the non-chasers, the fighters, the slow dogs, the unemployable ones, the ones whose bodies have left them minutely unfitted for their job. Using simple words which stretch like careful bridges across a turmoil of feeling, the letter suggests that the homes should be paid for by the sport, and that 'buildings, paddocks and play areas be made available'. This is the place at which the fun, the worldliness, the life and the larks of greyhound racing drain away from me like spent adrenalin. When I read that twenty-year-old plea, those poor little words 'play areas', I want there to be no dogs in the world to disturb the accumulations of my adulthood with their eyes like black tears. This is the burden that the dog man carries around with him, which keeps his heart childlike and his hand reaching gently towards the ears of his greyhound. It is the knowledge that there is a moment in the life of all these dogs when their dual identity – their public and private personae, if you like – will become irreducibly single. So long as they are racing, these greyhounds are viable, they are commodities, they are workers, they are players in the world; but they are also, always, only dogs, and that truth, always known but not always acknowledged, eventually becomes the whole truth. The respect that the dogs are accorded, for their usefulness, for their earning power and their ability; the self-containment that one sees in them while they are pursuing their careers – suddenly these will drop away, leaving them entirely dependent, entirely vulnerable. For some, un-protected in their mediocrity, this moment comes almost immediately. For most, it comes after four or so years hard work. For others, a few others, shielded by their armoury of talent, it will come only at the very end. But it will come: to Indian Joe, the black, the beautiful, the nonchalantly powerful, dying on a sofa in Ireland at the age of ten; to Commutering, slipping into the arms of a kindly vet. I preserve my sporting greyhounds in moments that exist without past or future. Indian Joe rolling his casual eye at the worshipping Derby crowd. Commutering raising his ears into their tall triangles. These are images, like Hamlet staring into the eyes of a skull, upon which time has converged. I cannot connect the memories that I have of these dogs – memories of moments of what is, for me, their eternal prime – with the knowledge of their quiet and powerless deaths.

But these were lucky greyhounds. They were surely luckier than Patricia's Hope, for example*; my memory of him cannot be fixed at some point of timeless triumph, for I know too much about his future beyond the moment when he won his second Derby. I cannot think of him as the greyhound that equalled the record of Mick the Miller. This is how I think of him: in 1980, at the age of ten, he had been sent from Ireland to White City to take part in a parade of champions. The GRA had paid his owner for his return flight, but when the dog reached Dublin, the man refused to give the money to the airline. Patricia's Hope was sent back to Heathrow, where he was found, abandoned. He was lucky enough to be rescued and taken to Hook Kennels. After a time he was discovered to be suffering from a wasting disease. He was nursed through the last years of his life, and is buried in the Hook grounds. But after all those years of attention and worship, after standing twice upon that rostrum to receive the greatest honour in his sport, after returning for his parade of champions to the arena of his triumphs, after hearing again the forgotten yet familiar acclaim of a crowd; to be thrown into the confusion, the bewilderment, the cruelty, the uncaringness of a world that he thought to be his admirer – one can scarcely think of it.

Who was this man, who marked Patricia's Hope 'return to sender' and subjected him to hour upon hour of unfamiliar terrors? What are such people? They are not dog men; they are the worst kind of imposter dog men, for to them greyhounds are nothing more than the repository into which they cram their selfish desires. What of the man who recently had his Walthamstow grader destroyed – no attempt to find it an alternative home – after it was disqualified for fighting? Walthamstow, to its credit, barred the man thereafter as an owner; so it cannot have been the unnamed track which advised another owner, whose pup was too slow to grade, that it could arrange for the dog to be put down. Yes, it happens, although nobody will admit how often it happens. These may be dogs, but they are dogs with a job to do, and only when they can do that job are they protected from a world which – for all their seeming self-sufficiency – they have no choice but to trust. What does happen to them? What can happen to them, when they are unemployable? Sometimes the NGRC's Retired Greyhound Trust will find homes for them; sometimes the tracks, about twenty-five of which run homefinding schemes, will do so; sometimes they are taken to Battersea, where I have seen them haunting small pens like the ghosts of their palmy youth. Sometimes their owners will keep them; sometimes they will pay their trainers to keep them; and there are some good, kind trainers who keep them anyway. Sometimes they are returned to their breeder, as my father's dogs often are. 'But I sell a lot of them, those that aren't going back to Ireland, because I don't want the worry of them when they stop racing. I don't want to know what happens to them. I'm not completely heartless. I'm semi-heartless.' Does that sound callous? – I suppose it must do, but I know that it is not. I know that it is my father, grappling gruffly with the unanswerable problem at the heart of his sport, trying, as I do, to keep his relationship with the dogs elliptical and bearable, his memories of them fixed at the point upon which time converges.

One cannot help but wish that the extra £3 million that the NGRC hopes soon to receive from the off-course bookmakers were to be spent on the welfare of the greyhounds, rather than, as is presently being suggested, on the dope test. Of course £3 million wouldn't go very far; but somehow that is scarcely the point – the lives of the dogs after they have finished racing should be of as much concern to the sport as their lives when they are actively serving it. They are not, and probably they never will be. And yet the twenty-year-old plea for greyhound homes has, in a small way, been answered. It is only one home, and it can only house about sixty dogs, but it is the creation of an individual who, in her refusal to accept that there is nothing to be done about the unanswerable problem at the heart of her sport, puts most of those connected with it to shame.

At the end of a country lane in Essex there is a small cluster of racing kennels, the last of which is kept by Johanna Beumer – teacher, dog woman, heroine – for the housing of unemployable greyhounds. Some of the owners of the dogs pay for them to live in these kennels and come to visit them every Sunday, but others have simply been abandoned: Johanna Beumer told me of how, recently, a man had casually drawn up in a car, dumped three old dogs and driven swiftly off again. Most of the money that pays for the keep of such greyhounds, and for the wages of a kennel manager, comes from a fundraising evening at Walthamstow (some other tracks run similar evenings, raising money in order that the Retired Greyhound Trust may pay trainers to keep ex-racers in their kennels). Fired by the courage and determination of the righteous, Johanna Beumer will raise perhaps £10,000 in this one night; she will find a sponsor for every race, and for every dog that runs in every race; she will pass round collection boxes; she will invite celebrities; she will parade before each race two of her greyhounds, one of which is homeless, one of which has been homed – for this is really her objective, to find homes for these dogs, to keep baling out her kennels lest they sink under the weight of all these unemployables, these ghost greyhounds.

On the day that I visited, a dog man was there who had driven all the way from Wales to take away with him a greyhound of about six years of age. He and I had walked the aisles of the kennels, stretching out hands towards the ancient dogs, whose eyes bore down like tired reproaches upon their spindle faces; towards the recent racers, who still looked charged and viable, impassively bewildered as they stood in the limbo world between their two different lives; towards the useless two-year-olds, whose lively bodies had no knowledge that they had been saved from a premature death. Here now, at the place where the dogs are known only as Bella and Walter, as Henry, Windsor and Tramp, where their racing identities had been forgotten – I asked the kennel manager about one or two of them, and he simply couldn't remember the names under which they had run – here is the place in which the pure heart of greyhound racing was born.

As I drove away from the place, I was thinking of the pure heart, and of the lary body that so loudly smothers it. The lary body, and the electric shimmer of the clothes that it wears. The world that it inhabits: a venal world of corrupt materialism, but also one of warm generosity, in which rich explosions of laughter spread a coarse bloom of humanity, in which sense is valued above sensibility, in which life is marvellously simplified – the philosophy being that money is all, that without money there is nothing, but that even money is no good to you if it makes you boring, if it makes you miserable, if it makes

you cruel, if you *don't know how to enjoy it*. The world of
the lights around the stadia; of the Saturday night boys
at Walthamstow; of the Derby roar, the wall of sound
built by gamblers; of the bookmaker, with his shrewd-
eyed smile and leather overcoat, bunging a score to his
little legman; of Al Burnett and his two dazzling Pigalles;
of Barney and Alfie and their £30,000 dog; of scams,
and coups, and tickles; of fun, and laughter, and nights
out; of the real men in the real and adult world. Two
perfect dog days, earlier this year. One: I had gone with
my father to the 1992 Derby semi-finals, where we ate in
the restaurant and where, to my father's very faint irrita-
tion, I won over £100 by getting up two trios*. For the
first hour or so the early summer sun flooded the vast
glass frontage of Wimbledon stadium; then it stepped
aside, leaving the stage to the business of the night.
Frank Melville came to our table and we talked about
the night's racing – was Farloe Melody due to win? did
Glengar Ranger stay? was it far enough for Winsor
Abbey? – and then, elliptically, mingling the present with
the past, we talked about Jerry H, about Commutering,
about the day that Frank had told my father that, yes, he
could take his dogs away if that was what he wanted, but
he needn't think he was having their leads; serenely,
delightedly, we played with the feeling of being dog
people. As the best greyhounds in the country paraded
around the track, a collection box for Johanna Beumer's
dogs circulated the stadium, within it a huge nest of £5
notes. As I returned from wandering around the bars
and placing one of my triumphant trios, a man handed
me a Tote ticket, on which was written in tiny script:
'My name is John Please ring me at my shop in Wool-
wich between 10.30 5.30 tom on 081-000 0000 P.S. I

would love to have your company here tues nite.' This man found me on a later wandering and asked me whether I was going to telephone him. I shrugged my helpless and apologetic no. 'Ah well, I'm used to backing losers,' he said.

Two: the Sunday morning after the Derby final, I was again with my father, in the pub, after visiting the dogs. We were drinking with my father's trainer, and with a dog man who was telling my father that one of his Jerpoint greyhounds, a dog just capable of winning A1 races, should be entered for the Derby next year. 'You reckon, do you?' said my father, as laughter threatened like rain. 'I do reckon. He's as good as plenty that were in it. I tell you what, he could get to the final. I would bet you that, next year, you would want to enter him for it.' At which point some, at least, of the laughter had to be let out. The man, impregnably contained within his own logic, began to tighten, shout and jostle with the rage of the assailed self-righteous. 'Farloe – you talk about Farloe,' he said. 'What got done worst of all at the first bend last night?' For some reason – perhaps thinking he would then be able to go on and answer himself – he had addressed this question to me. 'Two,' I said. 'Forget Two,' he said. 'What got done worst of all, that could have won it, that was in a position to win it?' 'Five,' I said. 'Ah,' he said, with the air of one who had arrived at his true destination. 'Five. If Five hadn't got done like that at the first bend, Five would have won it . . .' 'But Five and Six got done, if it comes to that,' I said. 'Farloe didn't get a clear run. Didn't they knock each other?' 'That five dog would never have beat Farloe,' said my father. 'Wasn't fast enough. It got a flier, else it wouldn't have been at the races with Six. That six dog's a hell of a greyhound. I shan't be running my dog against him, whatever you say about him . . . ' And then the laughter really did erupt. 'Ah well, you say that,' said the dog man. 'You say that.' There was a pause. Chuckles rippled silently. Then he started again. He wanted to sulk, but he couldn't stop dog talking. 'Anyway, it's a bloody disgrace, running the Derby at Wimbledon. This is supposed to be the best race, and you've got every bloody greyhound in it getting knocked. It's a bloody disgrace.' 'Well, that is quite true,' said my father. 'The only one that missed it all was the four, because it walked out of the traps. I mean, that one dog, he stood no chance, really, with the two outside of him. And the three got out, which it never does.' 'Three moved to the rails,' said my father's trainer. 'I think that maybe caused some of the trouble. No, but Farloe would have won it.' 'But what I'm saying is,' said the dog man, 'there shouldn't be all that trouble in a Derby final! They should run it at Wembley, in my opinion. It shouldn't be run at that track at all, is what I'm saying.' 'Can't run it at Wembley,' said my father. 'Wembley's got all the bloody American footballers and bloody pop groups to contend with. Half the time you got no racing at Wembley.' 'But what I'm saying is they shouldn't run it at Wimbledon. They should not. It's bloody diabolical. It's not the same race since it's not been run at White City.' 'Ah well, now you're talking,' said my father.

These two dog days – nothing to them really, just dog talk, just feeling myself a part of something, a man's world, a real world – connect with and even symbolise other moments in my life, moments when I have felt the acrid bloom, seen the fallible smile and heard the forgiving laughter of adulthood all around me. Afternoons drinking with ageing bohemians in Soho bars. Afternoons finding the Derby winner at Epsom. New Year's Eve in my grandmother's pub. Occasions which hum and throb with atmosphere, which are opaque with smoke, which smell of wine and beer, which are gallant and ordinary and human, which say that life itself is the only thing that matters, which are bittersweet because, even as they celebrate a moment of life, that moment is dying and they are toasting its mortality.

Which apprehension of pain within pleasure leads me back into the pure heart of the dogs, and the feelings that it holds which make it too sensitive to touch. The moments that arouse those feelings: my father turning his back on me after Commutering's death, saying 'I wasn't going to do that to the old feller'; Patricia's Hope blinking up at the closed faces of the Heathrow travellers; the salty muzzle of the old black bitch at the kennels, held at her owner's hip; the honey brindle pup trotting by my side, head in the air, like a thin and tiny horse; Jerpoint Joey stumbling slow and submissive, trusting and accepting; eyes in my eyes; paws at my arms; memories of the eternal prime; knowledge of the slow decline; the dogs, the dogs. Again these moments symbolise other moments in my life, moments when I have had the heart of vulnerability revealed to me. Sudden visions of my family – my father's hands, my mother's smile, a photograph of my brother as a child – in which they seem unguarded, unprotected. Sudden glimpses of the love in men, red-faced and choking back tears before the wise grey nods of Desert Orchid, the third Grand National of Red Rum – which apprehension of innocence within cynicism leads me back to the lary body of the dogs.

And so I realised the unresolvable paradox within the world of greyhound racing: one might even say within the world itself: that neither the pure heart nor the lary body is more powerful than the other. At times it will seem that one is more powerful, but it will not be so. At the 1992 greyhound awards dinner dance at the Hilton Hotel, I sat amid the dog men, hilarious with drink and with the roaring earthy feel of the occasion; at one point in the evening I left the ballroom and found Murlens Abbey, the dog that had won the Greyhound of the Year award, standing shivering and overwhelmed in a small and seething foyer. Not just I, but almost every person that passed him, was impelled to fondle his blue-and-white head. Our pure hearts bled a little as we did so. Something in us would have forgone the party to sit quietly with him and soothe his barely contained terror; and something else in us yearned towards the fiery brandies, the worldly banter, the brilliantly lit ballroom to which, when we returned, we would take the thought of that dog, vulnerable and shaking inside his red and gold winner's coat. The pure heart and the lary body are in balance, and in conflict, with one another. Each contradicts the other; yet each protects the other. The pure heart would bleed to death without the lary body; but the body would be hollow, cold, meaningless, dead also, without the heart.

I had thought that was the end – nothing more that I could say. And there isn't, except that these are only words, attempting to hold onto things which will always run away from them. While I was writing them I got a phone call from my mother telling me that one of the dogs was dead. Feeling nothing, as one doesn't for a moment, I simply asked her which one it was. She didn't say anything. 'Is it Ali?' I said, my mind now grinding and whirring as I tried to imagine what had happened to her. 'No, it's Laura,' she said.

Laura was one of the pups that I had watched with my father on that summery Sunday when the air had swelled with promise; the one that had been named after me, the huge long skinny black bitch that I had walked the week before. The last time I had seen her she had been standing in habitual lupine pose, silky reptile head hanging down between her front paws as she scrabbled hopelessly for the Maltesers that I had tried to put into her mouth. A few days after this she had been trialling at Oxford and had, I don't quite know, couldn't ask for details, run into a wall or a post and had, again I assume, broken her neck. Anyway she was dead. She had never exactly grown up before she died, I felt; each week I expected her lanky frame to have filled out but it didn't ever seem to; nor did she ever, after her initial burst of nervous zest, seem to have settled in England. Each week I found her head low, her temperament unstable, her big body trying to find its own ease. 'But I think she might be really good eventually,' I said to my father, and I believed it. I believed that when her limbs collected themselves together and her body became sleek, then she might be something extraordinary. It was so rare to find a bitch of that manly size and wolfish conformation that I felt there had to be a reason for it. I had said as much to my father. 'Well, she could be anything, that one,' my father had said.

Dog racing loves life. It is a celebration of life forces: expectation, hope, desire, greed. Its lary body wants to enjoy. *I* want to enjoy. I want to inhabit that adult world that I first saw as a child. I want the real world of the dogs in my life forever.

Yet its pure heart, and my pure heart, cannot escape the spectre of a big black baby of a dog crashing eagerly towards its own obliteration. The image hits my mind with the same force that Laura hit the wall. When I first heard about it, I hated the fact that I had made material out of this cruel thing. Then I wanted to write about Laura; then I hated myself for making material out of her. Most of all I hated the fact that I had just written all those lines about the deaths of racing dogs, forgetting that, even as I was writing them, the thing that I was describing was still happening. Then I thought that I could write that feeling as well. I do think of it as an honest sort of tribute to a dog that, otherwise, would not only never be remembered, but would never be known to have lived at all.

What else is there to do? What difference would it make it I were to stop loving greyhound racing, to let the blood of the pure heart overrun the lary body? Like life, sport is a continuum, a cycle in which it seems that endings need not be confronted – although one always knows that they are there – because there are always more beginnings. I remember when Desert Orchid failed in his attempt to win a fifth King George VI Chase, and sport demanded that Channel 4 Racing choose, for its final screen image, a shot of a six year old horse, warm and dank with the newness of victory, and not an image of a deposed and serene emperor, a riderless galloping grey. It shocked me for a moment, but what else could have been done? Sport goes on, life goes on, I will buy *The Greyhound Life* tomorrow to see how two of Laura's brothers ran (do they miss her? I think they probably do, but they are now part of that remorseless adult world as well). And I will still hope that they have won tonight, and still hope that a new litter of pups is being groomed for greatness in Ireland, and when I return to the kennels on Sunday I shall see a black shadow prowling its pen with its head hanging down like a wolf's, and remember when that shadow was itself a vessel of hope.

Notes

Chapter 1

Page

12 even money: tight bookmaking odds in which a greyhound is reckoned to have a 50-50 chance of winning a race.

13 ten classics: the Cesarewitch (Belle Vue); the Derby (Wimbledon); the Gold Collar (Catford); the Grand National (Hall Green); the Grand Prix (Walthamstow); the Laurels (Wimbledon); the Oaks (Wimbledon); the Scottish Derby (Shawfield); the Scurry Cup (Catford); the St Leger (Wembley).

13 *The Greyhound Life*: daily supplement with *The Sporting Life*.

15 37 tracks: Belle Vue (Manchester); Brighton; Bristol; Brough Park (Newcastle); Canterbury; Catford (London SE6); Cradley Heath; Crayford; Hackney (London E15); Hall Green

(Birmingham); Henlow; Hull; Middlesbrough;
Mildenhall; Milton Keynes; Monmore
(Wolverhampton); Norton Canes; Nottingham;
Owlerton (Sheffield); Oxford; Perry Barr
(Birmingham); Peterborough; Portsmouth;
Powderhall (Edinburgh); Ramsgate; Reading;
Romford; Rye House; Shawfield (Glasgow);
Stainforth; Sunderland; Swaffham; Swindon;
Walthamstow (London E4); Wembley;
Wimbledon (London SW17); Yarmouth.

16   NGRC registration: the flat fee for registering a
      greyhound is £20, plus a £3 administration fee. If
      a dog is bred in Ireland then an additional £10 is
      paid to the Irish Coursing Club. £5 of each
      registration fee goes to the Retired Greyhound
      Trust, a charity formed by the NGRC in 1974 to
      help owners and trainers find homes for ex-
      racing dogs.

20   £25 – a pony; £500 – a monkey.

20   place: a bet in which a dog is backed to run
      second.

20   forecast: a bet in which one attempts to pick both
      the winner and the second in a race – the most
      popular bet on the Tote, because it can't be
      made with an on-course bookmaker.

21   10 per cent betting tax: of course, one does not
      have to pay 10 per cent of one's stake when

placing a bet in a shop. One can elect instead to pay back 10 per cent of one's winnings, should there be any.

23   blue: blue dogs are beautiful and unusual, but they are not popular with dog men as they are generally considered to be of suspect character; although if one were to question a dog man about why he mistrusts blue greyhounds, he would simply say that blue greyhounds are not to be trusted. This is one of the many pieces of received 'wisdom' that make up the lore of dog racing.

Chapter 2

Page

33   lary: a marvellous word, once featured on *Call My Bluff*. It was unknown to all those dinner-party-guest contestants but would be recognised by any dog man, Cockney, etc. According to my dictionary it is of Australian provenance; but I cannot think of it as anything but a London word, a conflation of the words leery, wary and garish. It is a millionaire market trader, it is a bright gold Rolls-Royce, it is a country mansion in Wanstead, it is the good-humoured smile and suspicious eyes of a successful bookmaker. An

acquaintance of my father, who had been in the
business of selling food out of the back of a van,
eventually made quite a lot of money from his
trade and started flashing it around: rings, red
polonecks, declamatory suits, dainty house
ornaments, a condom-shaped car. 'He used to be
a silly old sod,' said my father. 'Now he's a silly
lary old sod.'

33   Harringay: greyhound stadium near Tottenham
in north London. Demolished in 1987.

35   the Stow: Walthamstow stadium.

47   *The Greyhound Magazine*: essential monthly
reading for dog men, it was founded in 1968 and
merged with the monthly newspaper, *The
Greyhound Star*, in 1986. It contained analyses of
the current racing scene, reminiscent essays and
page after page of advertisements for stud dogs.
Its front cover was often a colour photograph of
some crack greyhound being fondled by a comely
girl in a halter-neck top and platform shoes ('. . .
London model Froggie is pictured with Jimmy
Adams' top Romford greyhound Hopping
Champ . . . Froggie is currently engaged on *The
Benny Hill Show* . . .'). Although *The Star* is
similar in content to *The Greyhound Magazine*, its
form does not have the same reassuring charm.

Chapter 3

when one thinks that these would be their very
first runs around tracks, a very reliable one.

Chapter 4

Page

74 running with heart: when Mick the Miller's body
was prepared for display in the Natural History
Museum, it was discovered that his heart
weighed 1½ ounces more than is usual for a
greyhound.

75 1973 National: Crisp, a stalwart old horse who
had made most of the running in the Grand
National, and who had a huge lead at the last
fence, was caught at the winning line by the then
upstart Red Rum.

76 two Derbies: Patricia's Hope equalled Mick the
Miller's record when he won the 1972 and 1973
English Derbies.

78 Seldom Led: Mick the Miller had been bought
after his 1929 Derby win for 2,000 guineas.
Seldom Led was bought for £5.

82 Ascot Suite: an enclosure for private parties
within Walthamstow Stadium.

85 Skimpot: a flapping track in Bedfordshire.

90 A6 Murder: a *cause célèbre* of the early 1960s, in
which a gunman hijacked the car of a courting
couple, forced the man to drive a meaninglessly
circuitous route towards the A6 near Bedford,
then shot both the man and his girlfriend. He
was killed and she was permanently paralysed.
Petty criminal James Hanratty was hanged for
the murder in 1962, but there is still doubt about
his guilt; Peter Alphon had been the police's
original suspect and has confessed to the crime
on many occasions, although his guilt has
remained unprovable also.

92 BBC: the BBC did relent to the extent of
broadcasting the occasional race on the radio,
showing the Derby on television until the closure
of White City in 1984 and inaugurating the
Television Trophy, which is still shown on
Sportsnight. But the relaying of races today is
done almost entirely by the deregulated media:
0891 phone numbers, SIS (Satellite Information
Services) live broadcasts shown in betting shops,
the Derby on Sky Television.

96 effects of evening betting shop opening: in the
first three months of evening opening, from April
to June 1993, attendances at NGRC tracks
dropped by 0.5% compared with 1992.

97   £3 million: in the 1992 Budget, Chancellor
      Norman Lamont reduced the Government share
      of the off-course betting tax from 8% to 7.75%.
      He expressed the hope that the extra revenue the
      bookmakers would gain by this ¼ per cent cut
      would be passed on to both horse and greyhound
      racing. The latter's share of the ¼ per cent
      works out at about £3 million. The bookmakers
      have, after some discussion, declared themselves
      willing to pass this money on to greyhound
      racing, which means that the sport would, as of
      1993, receive around £6 million a year from the
      off-course betting industry: a 100% increase. At
      the time of writing, the bookmakers and the
      British Greyhound Racing Board (the sport's
      non-profit making representative body) are
      discussing the formation of a committee which
      would oversee the spending of the money.

97   mid-1980s: in 1984, greyhound racing
      attendances dropped below 4 million. Only the
      combined effect of the newly-businesslike
      attitude to the organisation of the sport, and the
      publicity of all those colour supplement articles
      headlined 'Going to the Dogs', brought
      attendances back above that figure in 1987.

Chapter 5

Page

111   Lively Band: had a funny eye, I always thought,
       but he had never actually fought until this race. It
       must have seemed to the dog men as if
       humorous little demons were riding the
       greyhounds round the track throughout this
       Derby and inciting them to do things that they
       had never done before. However, there was an
       'official' explanation for Lively Band's disgrace,
       just as there was one for Tartan Khan's triumph:
       he had been put to stud (was indeed one of the
       best sires of the seventies) after winning the Irish
       Derby and, it was seriously suggested, the shock
       of being taken away from his gigolo life and sent
       back to work had put the dog into an evil temper.

111   Consolation Derby: instigated in 1935 for the
       losing semi-finalists, which – due to the nature of
       the sport – can often be 'better' greyhounds than
       the qualifiers.

114   long odds: Duleek Dandy won in 1960 at 25/1.

Chapter 6

Page

122   John C: not his real name.

127   Del: not his real name.

134   Following the NGRC inquiry into the
      'Romfordgate' scam, Simpson was warned off
      from all NGRC stadia indefinitely; while
      Coughlan and Foley had their licences
      withdrawn indefinitely.

136   Rich: not his real name.

136   Jim: not his real name.

137   Mick: not his real name.

139   put the price down after the bet: this is why,
      when punters have their bet with a bookmaker,
      they announce what return they will get should
      they win: to confirm the odds before they are
      changed.

140   penciller: records all the bets for the bookmaker.

141   Dennis: not his real name.

148   nap: considered to be the surest bet of the
      meeting.

155   Jerry H: not his real name.

Chapter 7

Page

179   Frank Melville: one of my father's trainers at
       Hook Kennels, now a senior stipendiary steward
       with the NGRC, he won several major opens
       with his Harringay dogs and the classic Grand
       National in 1975. He was once spotted in the bar
       at White City by dog man Stan Bowles, then one
       of the most famous footballers in the country.
       'Look,' Bowles was heard to whisper, awestruck,
       to his companion, 'that's *Frank Melville*.'

192   four Derby winning bitches: Greta Ranee in
       1935, Narrogar Ann in 1949, Dolores Rocket in
       1971, Sarah's Bunny in 1979.

194   Ballyregan Bob: died in 1994. His trainer,
       George Curtis, received letters of sympathy
       from all over the world. On June 4th 1994, to
       the astonishment of the dog world, Bob lost his
       world record when an American greyhound, Pet
       C Rendezvous, won its 33rd consecutive graded
       race in Florida. However, there is no doubt that
       the quality of Ballyregan Bob's opposition, and
       the track records that he broke, put his still-
       standing British record into a different class.

Chapter 9

Page

231   Patricia's Hope: the greyhound was no longer
owned by the father of the dog child I had met,
several years earlier, in the bar at the Hook
Kennels.

236   trio: a very satisfying, sometimes very lucrative
bet, in which one predicts the first three dogs in
a race.